I Could Hardly Keep from Laughing

"I need to warn you:
Under these clothes,
I'm wearing boxer shorts
and I know how to use them"
- Robert Orben

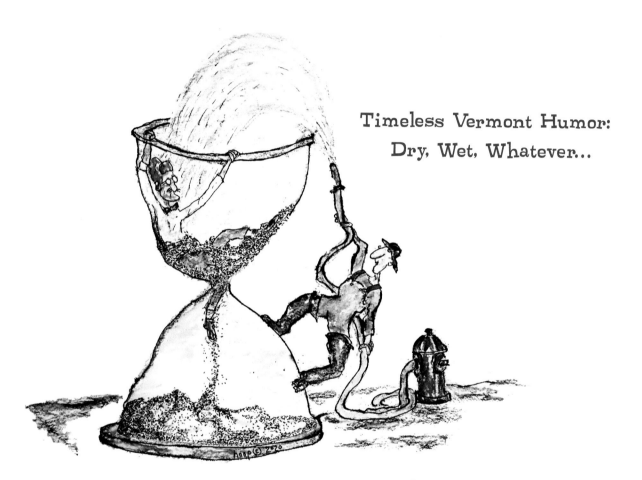

Timeless Vermont Humor:
Dry, Wet, Whatever...

Dry as Calvin Coolidge,
Soggy as Victory Bog

I Could Hardly Keep from Laughing:

An Illustrated Collection of Vermont Humor

To all the Droll don Hoop **Don Hooper and Bill Mares** Bill Mare

(Oh no, together again)

Foreword by Jeff Danziger

Rootstock Publishing

Montpelier, Vermont

Release Date: December 7, 2021
Softcover ISBN: 978-1-57869-060-2
Hardcover ISBN: 978-1-57869-081-7
Library of Congress Control Number: 2021905142

Published by Rootstock Publishing
an imprint of Multicultural Media, Inc.
27 Main Street, Suite 6
Montpelier, VT 05602 USA
rootstockpublishing.com
info@rootstockpublishing.com

Book design by Laughing Bear Associates, Montpelier, Vermont
Cover art by Don Hooper
Author photographs by Jan Peyser (Bill) and Jake Brown (Don)

Printed in the USA

ACKNOWLEDGMENTS

Allison, Sam, Jay, Miles and Daryll Hooper, Chris Hadsel, Timothy and Nicholas Hadsel-Mares, Dan Bolles, Andy Kovolos, Jane Beck, Paula Routley, Pamela Polston, Jordan Adams, Doug Wilhelm, Mason Singer, Stephen McArthur, Samantha Kolber, Courtney Jenkins, Jeff Danziger, Ed Koren, Al Boright, Bob Stannard, Alec Hastings, Anne Galloway, Frank Bryan, Peter Welch, Mark MacDonald , Lydia Wilcox.

Don's Dedication:

To my excellent friend and mentor Bill Mares who shepherded me into coloring these yarns for him. Bill assured me that winning at horseshoes was a noble but insufficient pastime.

Bill's Dedication:

To my father, Joe Mares, the first humorist I knew.

Herd any good ones lately?

CONTENTS (such as they are)

How ya doin' hibernating
in Vermont?

Chet completes Mavis' thought:

Oh the winters may be
long + hard,but...

But we make up for it
with Mud Season
and a two-day summer.

FOREWORD

Vermont humor is not cruel. It is not transient. It is not self-amused. It is not loud or slapstick.

Vermont humor is best defined by what it is not

by Jeff Danziger

An institutional humor, such as is found in Vermont, has to depend on widely, at least statewide, recognized straight lines. I once met Walter (Peanut) Kennedy standing in front of his car dealership in Chelsea. I pulled up, lost as usual, and asked him, "Where does this road go?" He looked at me a few seconds and then grinned. "You don't really want a serious answer to that, do you?"

Asking for directions is one of the enduring straight lines in Vermont. The approved answer to my question was something like, "It stays right here," or some variation. "Can I take this road to New York?" "Might as well, you've taken everything else."

Peanut was the Speaker of the Vermont House and ran for governor once. He brought some humor, not too much, to the legislature. "It's a good thing Vermonters don't get all the government they pay for," he once said. A little funny but as I say, not too much. And he didn't mind being the straight man.

In this state these straight lines depend on the general agreement that Vermont is poor, small, and beautiful. In addition, to live here at all is to prefer an acknowledged lack of opportunity to make money. You must be content to live simply, be content with small amounts, and rely on your own creativity. This may be lumped together in an attribute called "Yankeeness," spread across the northern New England states, combining undemonstrative passions, studied understatement, and a reverence for patient consideration. A Texan brags that he has so much land that he can get in his car and drive half a day without getting off his land. The Vermont farmer pauses and reflects that he used to have a car like that.

Grandmother is asked if it will rain. Well, she says, be a mighty long dry spell if it don't. And the general store that no longer stocks a certain brand of breakfast cereal. Why? Well, it sold too fast.

All of these, and countless others, are dry yet still a little elastic at heart. You might not think them actually funny for a few days, one day at least, and then on further thought worth a smile. I moved here in the seventies when what were called hippies arrived in Vermont. They came from New Jersey and California and Texas. They came mostly because they were

"It's a good thing Vermonters don't get all the government they pay for."
– Rep. Peanut Kennedy

dodging the draft by disappearing into the hills. Slowly but surely they dropped their city and suburban ideas about what was humorous and replaced them with slower but no less wise wit, the kind that needed a few days contemplation to get.

What the Vermont humor is best defined by is what it is not. It is not cruel. It is not transient. It is not self-amused. It is not loud or slapstick. If all those possibilities are removed, either intentionally or inadvertently, you wind up with a kind of pleasant observational strain, like the farmer who is told that with the Lord's help he has made a successful farm out of his rocky land. Yes, he says, but you should have seen this place when the Lord was running it by himself.

Vermont humor isn't all farmer wit. Most of what's funny here is the acceptance of how things are, and why, given the initial difficulties of weather, rocky soil, shortages and economic desiccation, people stay here. Most of what's in this book shows a background evaluation of what really matters in life. The funny stuff is on the surface but you have to be here to see why it is funny. In a way it defies description except to point out that Vermonters find each other amusing, even when they don't say anything. Silence, as a straight line.

The jokes and rousers here are also stunningly illustrated by former Vermont legislator and Secretary of State Don Hooper. He says he has given up politics to devote himself to the perfection of his cartooning skills, a prospect that fills me with competitive dread. At least he has a funny name—Hooper. Hah! Anyway, now I have to go practice bug eyes and big noses to get ahead of him. I once drew a really big nose, but an editor thought it was an enlarged spleen, and didn't think it was funny. All I am saying is, it's a tough business.

—*Jeff Danziger, political cartoonist, author,*
and recipient of the Herblock Prize and
the Thomas Nast Prize.

Hoopin' it up in Vermont

We start slow, then taper off

Warn't he funny!
Why, he was so funny, I could
hardly keep from laughing.

PREFACE(S)

In early 2018, Don asked Bill what his next book would be. Quick as lightning Bill said, "a history of Vermont humor, but only if you'll do it with me!"

We Start Slow, Then Taper Off

by Bill Mares

In the late 1800s, Mark Twain was invited to Brattleboro, Vermont, for one of his famous evenings of readings and humor. But, for almost two hours, he strained to raise more than a few smiles and a snicker. Baffled and a little annoyed, he finished early, left by the stage door, and sneaked around to the front entrance to listen to the departing audience. One elderly couple was getting into their buggy as the man said to his wife, "Warn't he funny! Why, he was so funny, I could hardly keep from laughing!"[1]

130 years later, Don Hooper and I are trying to keep up the tradition of taciturnity. When we met, thirty-five years ago, we were both first-term representatives in the Vermont legislature, from Brookfield and Burlington, respectively. We never served on the same committee, and Don stayed around Montpelier longer than I, but we shared an affection for the Capitol's denizens and ghosts.

In 1991, along with University of Vermont professor-buddy, Frank Bryan, we parlayed that fondness into a collection of true and almost-true stories about local and state politics in Vermont. I wrote a libretto about two custodians, Vern and Chet, who collected stories for *Out of Order: The Very Unofficial Vermont State House Archives*. Don did the art, and Frank oversaw the final product, which sold . . . modestly.

I went on to teach high school and write other books, and Don went on to higher office, becoming Vermont's secretary of state. During his term, he wrote a booklet on easing barriers to voting. From there he became New England Regional Representative for the National Wildlife Federation.

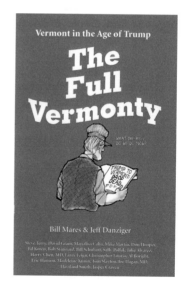

For the next three decades Don continued, like Edward Gibbon, to "scribble, scribble, scribble," and send to friends an irregular stream of cartoons from a host of fictitious card companies, while becoming bosom buddies with the celebrated *New Yorker* cartoonist Ed Koren, also a resident of Brookfield.

We stayed in touch, and when cartoonist Jeff Danziger and I assembled our eighteen-voice Vermont "choral" response to Donald Trump's 2016 election, *The Full Vermonty*, Don was a contributor.

In early 2018, Don asked what my next book would be. Quick as lightning, I said, "A history of Vermont humor, but only if you'll do it with me!" I'd set out to collect old and new stories, but with Don's cartoons, the book would be an anthology of something current, something loving and passionate, something original. Don set to work sharpening his colored pencils. After a couple years, the work was done.

When in Doubt, Mumble

by Don Hooper

Picking which funny people and stories to include in this book was a joyous chore. By contrast, having to choose which illustrations, and by whom, to accompany the yarns invited daytime nightmares, because Vermont has a plethora of great cartoonists, who are also friends. It came down to this:

1. Bill wants me on a solitary pedestal, to highlight my goofy style and occasionally disarming audacity.

2. Assuming any of Vermont's A-Plus illustrators would even want to appear in this book, I cowardly eschewed competition. Look at those prodigious talents! There's Vermont Cartoonist Laureate Ed Koren's *New Yorker* societal commentary; there's Jeff Danziger's syndicated clobber-'em-all political acumen; there's Tim Newcomb's deft finger on the pulse of Vermont. And that's without even considering Alison Bechdel, James Kochalka, and the cornucopia of gifted graphic artists emerging from James Sturm's Center for Cartoon Studies, in White River Junction. So, loading the dice for myself, we simply disqualified all other potential illustrators. Phew! No longer would we worry about snubbing anyone— we snubbed everyone.

3. Illustrating Vermont yarns and notions gave me a good project to reduce the guilt of "being retired," a euphemism for "aging in place."

Thanks, generous reader, for perusing this scramble of Vermontiana. It's kept Bill and me productive, perhaps even relevant, for another year.

We hope this collection will be both familiar and novel, comfortable and irreverent, collective and individual, whimsical and thoughtful, and altogether fun.

Proudly penurious Pascal was tighter than a brass screw in an oak floor.

If you come to a fork in the road
you really ought to take it.

CHAPTER 1

Dry, Wry, Understated

One of the first essays on Vermont humor, a monograph of forty pages, had neither date, publisher, famous author, nor even a place of publication. *Vermont Laughter,* by one Robert C. Davis, was as low-key as its format.

Davis's humor, learned from his farmer-father, was based upon two incompatible ideas: a sort of shock to the system, "a bounce in the brain that is pleasurable," and, in differing measure, jokes which relied on surprise, incongruity, and a lightning speed. The climax had to be whittled sharp.

It was a humor of scarcity and a joy in small things. And, if you're on the receiving end, it was the humor of ice picks, not meat cleavers. The old saying of parsimony, "Use it up, wear it out, make it do, or do without," could have been applied to Vermont humor.

As Davis wrote in his book, "The main elements were accent, timing, and subject matter—usually rural. The stories were well-paced, even aphoristic. The teller didn't wait for applause. Deadpan was an art form."

"Father's *fun* was jokes," Davis continued. "They didn't have to be new. He'd rearrange them, polish them. He'd sort them over, putting the prize numbers out in front. He and his peers were a breed of men who hankered for a nip of humor every so often. They craved it like a horse craves salt."

From *Vermont Laughter:*

- Busier than four hounds on one scent.

- So slow he would rot in his tracks.

- So dumb, if brains were dynamite, he wouldn't have enough to blow his nose.

Telling these jokes just to friends was a sufficient calling. Davis wrote, "How much better shaped and tasty were these homegrown jokes compared to those of a professional humorist pumping audiences for laughs! How tepid that performance when compared to the flash of flint upon steel within a man's own brain."

Davis claimed that understatement and the whopper [tall tales] are twins, opposite numbers, if you will. Both play with the truth, the one making it too little, the other too big. Neither is spontaneous, or a top-notch form of fun-making. "Understatement is the language of prudence. To be so flagrantly inside the truth as to arrest attention is about all that it can hope to accomplish."

Davis went on to say, "To make the gap between reality and the asserted fact as wide as possible, yet to retain a tenuous thread of plausibility, is the problem the composer sets himself. He can talk brash, but not wild. The risk he runs is that, in endeavoring to make the tale tall enough, he makes it labored."

"He and his peers were a breed of men who hankered for a nip of humor every so often. They craved it like a horse craves salt."

Example: "Ira said, 'I got a sure-fire way to catch fish, even when they won't bite. I take a plug of Day's Work chewing tobacco, cut it into little pieces and scatter them on the water. The fish eat the tobacco and when they come up to spit, I net 'em.'" [2]

✦

Davis celebrated the curative emotional power of humor. The laugh-provoking story became narrative scripture, and these stories circulated like currency of which there was little in fact and in metaphor, for he estimated the total number of jokes at less than one hundred. But, in the continual remolding, refinement, reassignment of dialogue and personnel, he said, "In the brains of those artists whose feet were following plows, whose hands were cutting corn, a joke might start out cocky in the morning and not be recognizable when it slunk home at night."

"Jim's wife eloped with the hired man!"
"Not in Jim's new Ford!?"

✦

One could say that Calvin Coolidge took Vermont's humor national. The 30th US president, arguably the most laconic, was once presented with a fine, handmade rake. The donor-orator gushed: "This hickory is like the president—sturdy, strong, resilient, and unbroken." Coolidge nodded his thanks, turned the rake over, and said, "Ash."

Vrest Orton, founder of the Countryman Press and the Vermont Country Store, and one of the founders of *Vermont Life* magazine, wrote: "The humor of the Vermonter, of which Mr. Coolidge was the classic exemplar, is dry, like the wine of the Graves region. It is also frugal. No words are wasted in explanation. It is dramatic, although unwittingly so. A Vermonter will relate a simple, innocent story which seems to have no point and is concerned only with common daily happenings. While you are pondering, suddenly the point will hit you. This device is the sturdy basis of all great comedy, since the days of the Greeks. Lastly, some Vermont humor may seem like a trick, often known as a practical joke, but it is never a dirty trick that hurts people, or leaves a sour, bitter taste."[3]

In the 1940s, Keith Jennison, a seventh-generation Vermonter who worked in New York advertising before starting his own publishing house, wrote two books in which he paired photos from the 1920s and 1930s with Vermont sayings and aphorisms. Jennison once told a *Vermont Life* interviewer, "The greatest humor, the lasting humor, comes from adversity. There are no answers, but it comes out funny."[4]

"Some Vermont humor may seem like a trick… but it is never a dirty trick that hurts people."

For example, one photo shows a man and a boy drawing water from a hand pump. The caption reads, "Sonny, how'd you find the horse that everybody was looking for?" The next photo shows a horse standing calmly beside a stone fence, with a caption that reads, "Well, I thought if I were a horse where I would go and I did and he had."

The 1950s brought a cadre of academic collectors of humor to Vermont, including Allen R. Foley, a professor at Dartmouth College, who lived in Norwich, Vermont; Francis Colburn, a professor of art at the University of Vermont; and Walter Hard of Manchester, Vermont, who was one of the founders of *Vermont Life* magazine.

Former Governor Deane Davis told a story of a visitor to Walter Hard's bookstore in Manchester:

> "How do you like Vermont?" asked the neighborly Hard.
>
> "Oh, I think it's a great place," the visitor said. "Beautiful and quiet. But you've got to admit, there's a lot of strange people up here."
>
> "Yes, that's right," said Hard, "but they all go home, come September."[5]

Or this, from Foley:

> "Does it matter which road I take to Goshen?"
>
> "Not to me, it don't."

✦

Then, in the 1960s, those visitors began staying.[6] In 1962, Vermont elected Philip Hoff, Vermont's first Democratic governor in a hundred years. The interstate system, IBM, and the back-to-the-land movement brought more newcomers. In the 1980s, Frank Bryan and I took advantage of the moment to pen *Real Vermonters Don't Milk Goats,* which documented the tipping point when the out-of-state "Flatlanders" would triumph over the natives. By the end of its run, the book had sold one copy for every ten of Vermont's 500,000 residents.

That was also the decade when Hollywood presented its version of Vermont to the nation through The Bob Newhart Show, a sitcom about a New York writer who moved to Vermont to run an inn. As Vermont cartoonist Jeff Danziger observed, "Vermont humor is a little bit bitter, a little bit at the expense of the outsider, but also gentle and self-deprecating." Of humor generally, he also said, "Everything is so twisted by television, that people stand there waiting for the laugh track to cue them."[7]

With the national significance of illustrators like Koren and Danziger, Vermont expanded its humor repertoire from dry and understated to a variegated full palate. But both Ed and Jeff regularly paid could-hardly-keep-from-laughing respect for Vermont understatement. Danziger, for example, adeptly drew the clueless tourist "from away" interrogating the roadside Vermonter about when the sought-after "peak foliage" would arrive in Orange County.

"Oh," deadpans the Vermonter, "just missed it. Peak passed through about fifteen minutes ago."

Or, "Do you have tofu?" asks the just-arrived hippie.

Al Floyd, proprietor of Floyd's Inconvenience Store, amiably responds, "Nope, but we got Dr. Scholl's."

That's deadpan Danziger.

✦

> **"Vermont humor is a little bit bitter, a little bit at the expense of the outsider, but also gentle and self-deprecating."**

In the 1970s, Vermont humor took to the stage in a variety of forms and venues. Norman Lewis, a school principal, created a fictitious character, named Danny Gore, who became a perennial candidate for governor, and brought the Northeast Kingdom to audiences around the state. In Woodstock, Vermont, Bill Boardman, a former teacher at the Yale School of Drama, assembled the Panther Players to perform skits and comedy with a broad national focus that was more biting than the Washington-based Capitol Steps. Author and cultural entrepreneur Bill Schubart and others satirized the state's popular promotional magazine with a single edition of *Vermont Lifer*.

In a spoof of Nashville's Grand Ole Opry, lawyer Al Boright and farmer George Woodard established their own "Ground Hog Opry" of comic routines peppered with potty humor, political jabs, fictitious products, and first-rate country music. From Stowe, Rusty DeWees developed a distinctive stage character called The Logger, after the "Antoine the logger" ("sheet a cat's ass") role he played in a production of

nature abhors a vacuum

David Budbill's hardscrabble *The Chain Saw Dance.* In Hardwick, locals put on full-blown vaudeville shows with plenty of humor. In their goofiness, they posed this unspoken question to audiences: Are people smart in a stupid kind of way, or stupid in a smart kind of way?

Here's an example from one of our former legislature buddies, Bob Stannard, of Manchester, who had a stage career as a harmonicist and humorist:

> Having loaded my first of what was to be dozens of truckloads of free wood from a landowner, I headed out of the somewhat damp woods to bring the wood home. I was with a friend in a bigger truck, who thought he should go first. He didn't. Meandering my way through the forest, I went through a wet spot that turned out to be more than wet, and got stuck. No problem, I thought, I'll just put a couple of sticks under the tire and I'll sail outta here.
>
> I knew I was in trouble when the last stick disappeared. I had to call Tate's Towing. Nothing worse than admitting defeat. Tate showed up, surveyed the situation, and said, "You're stuck."
>
> "I know," I said.
>
> "Are you in four-wheel drive?"
>
> "Yes," I said.
>
> "You do understand the principles of four-wheel drive, right?" I remained silent.
>
> "You use two wheel-drive to get stuck, and four-wheel drive to get unstuck. When you use four-wheel drive to get stuck, then you need Tate to get unstuck."

I asked how much for pulling me out, knowing it would be fifty dollars.

"Six dollars will do it? You're not going to tell anyone about this, now are you?"

"Not for fifty bucks, but for six dollars I am."

Bubba Lugnut vowed not to let the Perfect become the enemy of the Good.

"A joke might start out cocky in the morning and not be recognizable when it slunk home at night."

CHAPTER 2

The Farmer

In his book, *Vermont Laughter,* Robert C. Davis speculated about how Vermont's humor developed and was curated in the years before the automobile changed everything. It was the humor between friends and neighbors, over the fence and on the stoop. It couldn't be too harsh, but still needed a bite to it. Dairy was king, but its subjects were not rich. With over thirty thousand farms in hundreds of villages, most Vermonters, wherever they lived, would have understood the similes and metaphors of Vermont wit.

For Davis's hardworking farmer-father, crops, prices, and the movements of fellow townspeople were, of course, the mainstay of conversation, but the exchange of stories was the frosting on the cake. The fabricating of laugh-provoking yarns fed an intellectual hunger.

As Davis recalls, "Intellectually, father and his Vermonters were keen as traps. They carried no ounce of surplus fat, either physically or mentally. Theirs was heavy work, and always on the margin of privation. The farming they practiced was not the scientific affair of later times. To walk behind a plow, cut grain with a scythe, and cultivate corn with a hoe, is an occupation which leaves the brain free to range. But their brains needed to be gnawing on something. Some men schemed out trades or mechanical inventions. Others, like my father, practiced their intellectual calisthenics in revamping and refining their collection of witty anecdotes."[8]

Vermont's early tale-spinners didn't shy away from difficult subjects, like life, death, and matrimony:

> Sign on a druggist's window: "Hams and cigars, smoked and unsmoked."
>
> ---
>
> At the druggist, a wife speaks: "You write the directions plain on the bottles—what's for my husband and what's for the horse. I can't have anything happen to that horse before the spring planting's done."
>
> ---
>
> "Ordinary, I weigh a hundred'n forty pounds. But when I get my dander up, I weigh a ton."
>
> ---
>
> A Vermont farmer, after years of trying, wins $50,000 in the lottery. A neighbor asks him what he'll do with his winnings.
> "Oh, I guess I'll keep farming until the money runs out."
>
> ---
>
> Many years ago, a country newspaper sent notices to delinquent subscribers: "Your subscription has expired."
> Among the many returns, one read: "So's Clyde!"

"The humor of the Vermonter is dry…. It is also frugal."
– Vrest Orton

At the newspaper office, a widow asks, "How much do obituary notices cost?"

"Fifty cents an inch."

"Oh, we can't afford that. Father was six-foot-two."

STATIC

by Walter Hard

Jed Thomas wasn't what you'd call
A drinking man.
Probably if he had been
More regular in his drinking habits
The evidence of over-stimulation
Would not have been so conclusive.
As far as the records showed
Jed never drank at all
Except on the last day of the Fair.
On that day he did all his drinking for the year.
It only took a few good drinks of cider,
To produce the desired effect.

One year, there was so much trouble
With disturbance at the Fair

Farther were six two

They had constables and sheriffs
From several towns around the grounds.
Displaying bright badges, they mixed with the crowd.

Along late in the afternoon
One of them came on Jed Thomas.
He was standing by the race track
Hold to the fence with both hands.
He seemed to be trying to catch Something
Which was revolving rapidly,
But as soon as he let go of the fence
He immediately joined the rotating movement.

The constable approached Jed quietly
And, touching him on the shoulder, he said,
"Move along Jed, don't be standing here."
With some difficulty Jed got his eye focused
On the shining badge.
He spoke with an injured air:
"Moooove on, you shay,
Miser Sheruff, don' you shee
'Sall I c'n do
T' stay where I be?"[9]

> "Are people smart in a stupid kind of way, or stupid in a smart kind of way?"

THE VILLAGE IMBECILE OUT-SMARTS 'EM ALL[10]

Ira was not playing with a full deck, even he admitted that. But, on occasion, he could outfox some of the bigger minds in the village. Whatever the answer, it was clear Ira started early. Here are some examples:

> Ira was so proud when he bought his first toothbrush.
> "Will you have paste with it?" asks the druggist.
> "No. They're dirty, but they ain't loose!"

A local farmer was short of workers at the height of haying season. Against his better judgment, he asked Ira to help for a few days.

> "How much'll you pay me?" said Ira.
> "Every cent you're worth."
> "Nope. I want a little more'n that."

Hired at another farm, Ira was quick and prompt in putting away his tools and getting to the dinner table first.

   One afternoon he was in the field, raking hay with the other hands, and the job was going slowly. Finally, he pulled out his watch, glanced at it, and said, "Reckon we'd better hurry up to finish this job so's we can get back to the barn before it's too late for quittin' time."

It ain't perfect...

But it ain't plastic.

Ira had a dog named Hellonrats that stuck to him like glue. The dog had a much-scarred muzzle, which brought frequent queries. "He got that for being too conscientious," said Ira. "He followed a rat into a keg of nails."

The dog was a famous vermin destroyer, and several merchants tried to buy him, without luck.

"How much you want fer him," asked one of the town fathers.

"Fifty thousand dollars. That's my price," said Ira.

"Too rich for me," said the man.

A few days later, the man saw Ira without the dog and asked where it was.

"Sold it!" Ira said proudly.

"Holy Cow! How much?"

"My price!"

"Did you get cash?"

"Not 'xactly. But I did get two, twenty-five thousand dollar cats."

✦

Ira was not above out-foxing himself: Of another sale, he once proclaimed, "Yes, sir, I sold a cord of wood for the highest price a cord of wood ever sold for in the state of Vermont. Fifteen dollars. And if I'd known he wasn't gonna pay me, I'd a charged him eighteen!"

✦

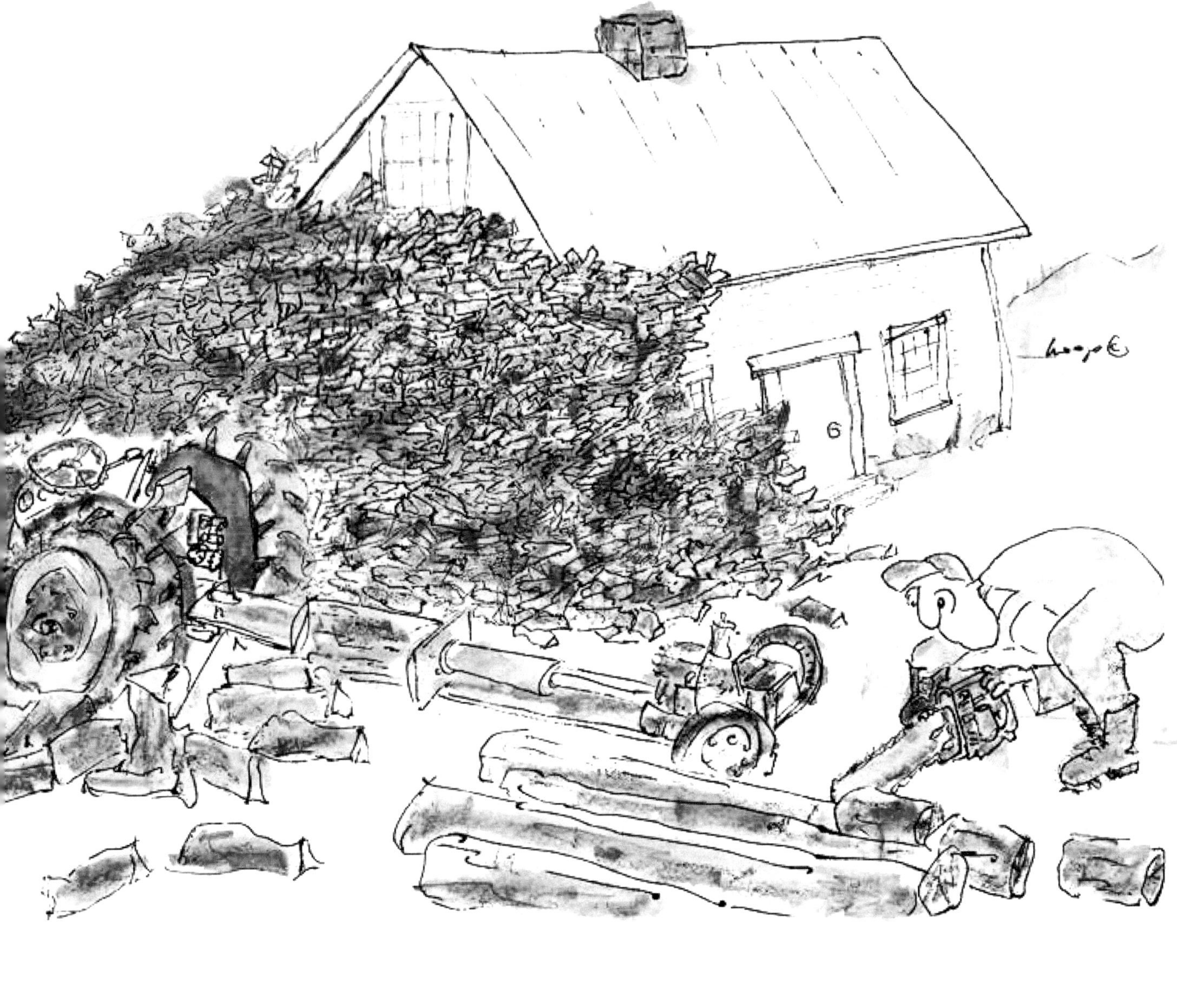

Walter Hard, a founder of *Vermont Life* magazine, and Allen R. Foley, a professor from Dartmouth, were to jokes what antique-pickers were to country auctions. They scoured store steps and cracker-barrel conversations for items they'd retail to city folks at a 100 percent markup. Foley collected two volumes of tales, *What the Old-Timer Said* (1971) and *The Old-Timer Talks Back* (1975).

✦

Foley claims he once came upon three farmers sitting on the country store stoop. He tried politely, then with some heat, to engage them in conversation. No replies.

"Is there some law around here against talking?" Foley asked acerbically.

"Nope, no law 'gains talking, but we prefer to keep our mouths shut until we're damn sure we can improve on the silence!"[11]

Foley went on: "A schoolboy in Corinth told me that last October, at school, he had recited his adopted version of the old jingle:

> As I was sitting in a shady nook,
> Along beside a babbling brook.
> I saw a lovely little lass
> Standing in water up to her knees.

"When I remarked that he didn't seem to have the right rhyme, he answered: 'That's what the teacher said, but I told her you had to remember we've had a helluva dry fall!'"[12]

✦

Said the bookseller to the farmer, "With this volume I'm offering you, you can make twice as much money."

The farmer replied, "No, thank you. I ain't farming half as good as I know how, right now!"

"Vermont humor is a little bit bitter, a little bit at the expense of the outsider, but also gentle and self-deprecating."

✦

A farmer bought a run-down farm, and with some very hard work, brought it back to more than passable shape. The local minister happened by one spring day, and marveled at the fruits of the farmer's labors.

"Isn't it wonderful what God and man can do when working together!"

"Ayup, that may be so," said the farmer, daubing sweat from his brow, "but you should have seen this place when God was working it alone!"[13]

OF DEATH AND DYING

Inscription on a cemetery stone, Stowe, Vermont:

"I WAS SOMEBODY.
WHO, IS NO BUSINESS
OF YOURS."

Another inscription, from Guilford, Vermont:

HENRY CLAY BARNEY, 82

"MY LIFE'S BEEN HARD
AND ALL THINGS SHOW IT;
I ALWAYS THOUGHT SO
AND NOW I KNOW IT."[14]

•

Two limericks from Vermont during the great influenza epidemic of 1918-20, when over seventeen hundred Vermonters died.

From the *Saint Albans Messenger*:

"A fly and a flea with the 'flu
Were quarantined so what could they do?
Said the fly, 'Let us flee.'
Said the flea, 'Let us fly.'
So they flew through a flaw in the flue."

From the *Brattleboro Reformer*:

"The fly and the flea with the 'flu,
Flew through the flue it is true;
But a flaw in the 'flu
With a chill turned them blue,
And the fly and the flea—they are through."

Socially Distance?
Masks? Huh?
You're kidding!
We nuzzle + hug.
We're Cluster Flies,
for Pete's sake.

A GOOD BARGAIN[15]

A farmer walked into the local bank and asked to borrow one dollar. Somewhat surprised, the teller said, "Of course."

"And the interest?" the farmer asked.

"Ten percent." [It was an earlier time.]

"Good," said the farmer. "And here's some collateral." It was a $1,000 US Savings Bond. The now-doubly mystified teller said this wasn't necessary, but he took the bond. The farmer left.

One year later, the farmer was back. He walked to the counter and plunked down a dollar and a dime. As the teller returned the bond, he asked the farmer, "Say, I don't mean to pry, but could you tell me why you wanted to borrow one dollar when you already had this $1,000 bond?"

"Well," said the farmer, "if I had put this bond in one of your savings boxes, it would have cost me ten dollars. This way, you only charged me ten cents!"

✦

Zeke had stomach cramps, which he was sure were caused by his wife's cooking. They doctor gave him a careful examination and asked the usual questions about his habits, food, and other things related to health. He gasped when Zeke told him how much tobacco he chewed daily.

"Why, Zeke, that's far too much!" he exclaimed.

"How much is too much, Doc?"

"Well, I would consider a plug a day as being excessive."

"Gosh, Doc, I drool more'n that in a day!"[16]

◆

A member of the hunting party had a worried look as he entered the lodge. He set his gun in the corner, hung his red hat, and took a glass of "chill medicine." He turned to his friends, and asked, "Is everyone here?"

One of the nimrods nodded, to which the first hunter replied, "Good! Then it must have been a deer I shot!"[17]

◆

While making his rounds in rural Vermont, the traveling salesman's car broke down, and he was forced to stay in a country inn. A fidgety man, he couldn't stay still and went out several times, each time returning more upset.

> "Where's the theater?" he finally barked at the innkeeper.
> "Ain't none," the clerk replied.
> "Well, you have a bowling alley or anything where a man can amuse himself?"
> "Nope," said the clerk.
> "Well, what in Heaven's name do you do up here for excitement?"
> "Up here, mister, we just don't get excited."[18]

◆

Once, Robert Frost was going fishing with two friends from Ripton. One arrived at the appointed hour, but the other, named Ira (pronounced Iree) Dow, was annoyingly late.

The exasperated friend burst out, to Frost, "That Iree Dow is as much slower than stock-still as stock-still is slower than greased lightning."[19]

ANOTHER FARM, OVER BACK[20]

by Vrest Orton

(In this poem, Orton writes as if he is his friend, Robert Frost.)

I

Robert, they tell me you bought another farm, over back.

What are you planning . . . to farm it?

No . . . I'd hate to think I was reduced to that.

They auctioned the place off, not many there;

I took it because nobody else bid.

It's lonely, hard to get to or from,

And the barn roof has fallen in.

II

Looks like a poor bargain to me.

You can make more money making stories.

That's the whole point; I got a story.

It came with the place.

Let me tell you:

Right after the auction, a little runt came up to me;

Wanted to know if I aimed to farm it. Like you.

(Everybody wants to get me back into farming, seems if.)

Said if I didn't, he'd kind of like to get some things out of my barn.

Wanted to know what I was asking for the drinking fountains,

Said they were built into the stanchions.

III

I suppose you gave them away.
You're always too generous.
No. I fooled you that time. I said to the fellow,
His name, I believe, was and most likely is, Mead . . .
If he hasn't starved himself to death by penury.
I said to him:—tell you what, Mr. Mead, I don't aim to farm it.
You go in there and take out the fountains . . .
Make up your mind what they're worth to you,
Then you pay me just half that amount.

IV

That seems pretty fair to me.
What did he say?
Well, he said, is that what you're asking, and I said,
That is what I am asking.
I have no need for drinking fountains. You take them.

V

What happened?
Nothing.
Not then. But a year later, Mead came around.
It was, in fact, last spring. He stood about where
You're standing now;
Overalls hitched up tight to tuck neatly into his rubber boots . . .
A little runt, not over five feet and bald as a beet.

He stood there, scuffing one boot back and forth
In the mud like a horse,
While he balanced on the other.
I waited.
If a man has got something to say,
I don't interrupt him.

VI

"Well," he hemmed for a spell . . . then he blurted out:
"Mister, seeing you don't aim to farm the place,
I don't know but if I might buy them drinking fountains."
Then he looked down sheepishly at the mud hole
His boot was digging and added:
"But they're so all-fired old, and hard to get out . . .
I don't know how I can afford
To pay what you're asking."

"But they're so all-fired old, and hard to get out...
I don't know how I can afford to pay
what you're asking."

Vermonters welcomed the out-of-staters' money, but not always their manners. Sometimes, Vermonters fought back, but with humor.

CHAPTER 3

Came to Play

As Vermont's population declined after the Civil War, the government joined the rest of New England in trying to entice people to tour the state, even to stay.

In contrast to the call of the wild mountains in New York and New Hampshire, Vermont sold itself as bucolic, with a focus on a pastoral, managed landscape: Here was a temporary escape from urban grit and grime, to a place of simplicity and virtue. The visitor might even buy an abandoned farm from a state-provided list. In 1911, Vermont's bureau of publicity's slogan offered "Vermont, Designed by the Creator for the Playground of the Continent." In 1946, the bureau became the Vermont Development Commission, which launched its quarterly promotional magazine, *Vermont Life*. By the mid-forties, 7 percent of Vermont's houses were seasonal.

About the same time, the ski industry took off, and, Vermont became a tourist destination in the winter as well as the summer. To help stimulate business in the fall, the state started to promote the foliage season, making Vermont a three-season destination. (Spring in Vermont goes unaffectionately by the label "mud season.")[21]

"The Beckoning Country… Vermont sold itself as bucolic… a place of simplicity and virtue."

Snow as a tourist attraction

In the 1960s, the state's simple and very successful slogan would be "The Beckoning Country."

Indeed, tourism brought lots of dollars to the state, and became the third leg of the tripod of Vermont's economy, the others being agriculture and manufacturing.

Not all interactions between visitors and natives were comfortable. Vermonters welcomed the out-of-staters' money, but not always their manners. Sometimes, Vermonters fought back, but with humor.

Francis Colburn, a native Vermonter whose day job was teaching art at the University of Vermont, wrote a fictional graduation address filled with "these fine old clichés, that bring tears to my eyes and I certainly hope you are going to water up some. This is a vanishing America that we want to preserve together."

In it, he told the story of two New York counterfeiters, who turn their trade to unconventional bills and decide to try out some eighteen-dollar bills on the storekeeper in Eden Mills, Vermont.

The pair entered the store and asked for a pack of cigarettes. "Tell me, my good man, can you change an eighteen-dollar bill?"

"Yes, I believe I can," said the storekeeper. "Would you like three sixes or two nines?"[22]

Got change for an Eighteen?

Sure. Do you want 2 Nines or 3 Sixes?

FAREWELL TO THE EMPIRE STATE

A Vermonter did well in the city and was about to realize his life's ambition —to return to the village of his origin. His wife was cold to the plan. The amusements and conveniences of town appealed more than the wide-open spaces. Nevertheless, she would be a martyr.

On the morning of their departure, everything was packed and their seven-year-old son was saying his prayers. The wife, with a gleam of triumph in her eye, beckoned for her husband to hear their child:

"Good-bye God, we're going to Vermont," said the child.

Pretending not to notice her smug smile, the husband said, "I wouldn't punish him if I were you."

"Punish him! Whatever for?" cried his wife.

"For profanity. Maybe you didn't hear what he said."

"And what was that?" asked his wife.

"Good! By God, we're going to Vermont!"

I'm not from Vermont—
but I got here quick as I could.

TEN-GALLON HUMOR

Relatively few Texans visited Vermont, but when they did, their braggadocio provided a barn-sized target for dry and crafty Vermonters. I know. I grew up in that land of Lone-Star bombast, where everything was bigger, even the insults.

"That ole boy is so dumb that if brains were gasoline, he wouldn't have enough to drive an ant's motorcycle around a bee-bee."

"He's so dumb, he thinks Jesus is still spelled with a small 'g'."

"He's so mean that if he played for the Hell Hounds, Coach Satan wouldn't even let him suit up for games."

Ready to take on anyone, the Texas bar brawler challenges the house: "You big SOBs line up, and you little SOBs, bunch up!"

A Texan visited Rutland and asked about a large building downtown.

"That's our City Hall. Ain't it magnificent?"
"In Texas, we have outhouses that big!"
Vermonter: "I don't doubt it a bit."

"Good-bye God, we're going to Vermont," said the child.

The Texas tourist, eyeing a farmer engaged in the Sisyphean task of removing rocks from his hill farm field, calls out: "What's ya'll doing?"

Jaw clenched, the farmer replies, "Pickin' up ruks!"

"Well, where did all the rocks come from" asked the tourist.

"Glacier brought 'em," hissed the farmer.

"Well, where did the glacier go?"

"Back to get more ruks!"

Finally, after the Texan had bragged about his state's low taxes, its physical size, the beauty of its women, and the number of cattle, oil wells, and guns, the bullied Vermonter shut him up by asking: "Well, mister, does Texas have the largest or the smallest jumbo shrimp?"

Where a classic Texas insult is: "He's all hat and no cattle," the Vermont equivalent is . . .

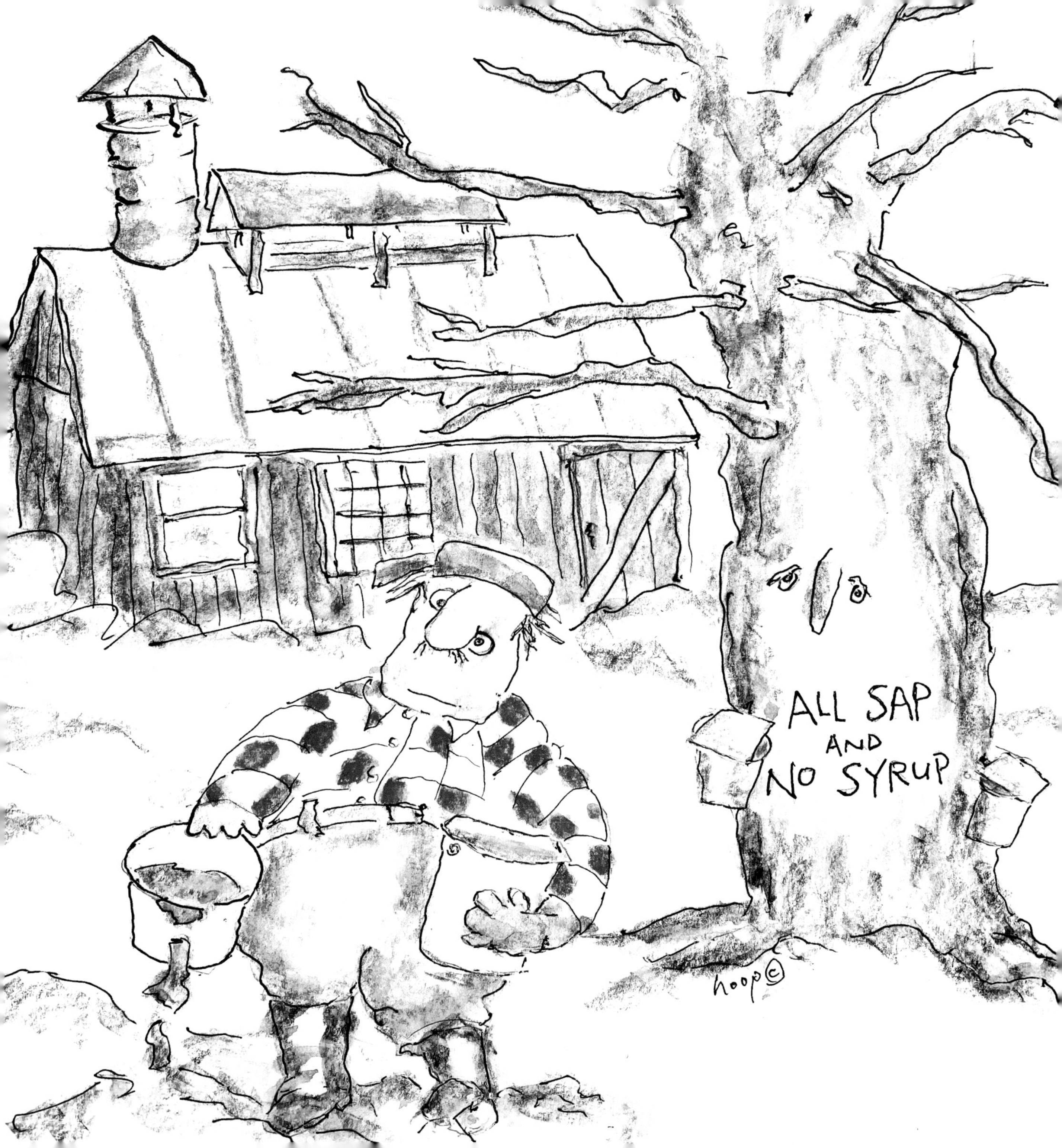
ALL SAP AND NO SYRUP
hoop©

SIGHTS OVER THE SIDE-VIEW MIRROR

How do I get to Barnard from here?
I wouldn't start from here.

Q. Can I get to Bethel from here?
A. Dunno.
Q. Well, is this the road to Randolph?
A. Dunno.
Q. Well, you don't know much.
A. I ain't lost.

STILL WORTH TELLING

"Howdy, Cal," said the man in one wagon passing another.

"Howdy, Newt!" the man in the wagon passed on, waving his whip.

"Cousin of mine," Vice-President Coolidge explained to a friend visiting Plymouth Notch. "Haven't seen him for twenty years."[23]

Q: How are the crops this year?

A: Not as good for a good year, but not so bad for a bad year.

Occasionally, my friends flatter me: they say I'm really "open-minded"

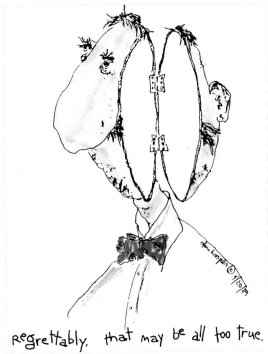

Regrettably, that may be all too true.

Q: The doctor thinks Uncle Pete's lost his mind.

A: He don't seem to miss it much.[24]

Q: You got your farm in such good shape, it could probably run itself.

A: Sure would, downhill.

Q: Most everyone here knows what's going on.

A: But they read the paper to find out who got caught at it.

Q: How long will it take me to get to town?

A: How fast are you going to walk?

Q: How much you get for them pigs you sold last week, Jesse?

A: Not as much as I figgered I might, But I never thought I would.

Q: What do you know today ... for sure?

A: Not a damn thing.

"Outside of a dog,
a book is a man's
best friend."
"Inside of a dog,
it's too dark to read."
— Groucho Marx

Country stores often had a large, round cheese under a glass dome. City folks rarely had seen one, because cheese was cellophane-packaged in urban stores.

A summer visitor was shopping in the general store one day, looking at the unusual variety of merchandise, and her eye fell on the cheese. The proprietor was standing near the counter, tasting a sliver. The lady tapped him on the back and asked, "Is that cheese?"

"No, ma'am, that's mah back."[25]

✦

A big, shiny Cadillac stopped in front of a country filling station, and the driver blew his horn loudly until an old man in dirty overalls limped out. The tourist said, "Listen, my car stops once in a while and then starts up again. I've had it in three city garages on the way up here, and they can't seem to find the trouble. I don't suppose you can fix it, but can you try?"

The old man lifted the hood and studied the situation a few minutes. He took out an old jackknife from his pocket, scraped a piece of metal, then went back to the garage for an oil can. After squirting a drop of oil, he shouted, "Start 'er up!" The engine roared, and then purred like a kitten.

The amazed tourist asked, "How could those experienced mechanics in the city, with their expensive equipment, fail and you found the trouble in a few minutes?"

The old man scratched his head and said, "Well, mister, when you ain't got no learning and no expensive gadgets, ye jest have to fall back on yer thinkin'."[26]

Clyde goes online.

✦

There was a time when the country stores in many resort places had two prices, one for the summer people who were considered rich, and another for the regular customers. One visitor became angry when she had to pay five cents more for a can of peas than someone else, who had just bought the same article. Unabashed, the storekeeper answered, "Well, you city folks come up here expecting we're goin' to skin ye, so we do. We might as well make a little profit as long as we bear the blame!"[27]

POKING THE SUMMER PEOPLE

by Loudon Young [28]

Way back here in the backwoods region of the Northeast Kingdom of Vermont, we have a strange seasonal phenomenon known as "Summer Folk." They are sometimes referred to by other names, but not all of them are printable. But anyhow, when the sidewalks of New York or Jersey become hot enough to fry eggs, they tend to blow out of there, and that's when they begin to arrive here. These people are difficult to describe. They come in all shapes and sizes, of most nationalities, and are of all ages. They all have a few things in common though, mainly gaudy shorts, sunglasses, time off, and more money than a lot of us. There, the similarities end, and to describe them further as a group would certainly do someone an injustice.

To us native Vermonters, the antics of some of these people reminds of the story about the New Jersey man, who, many years before we had

"We have a strange phenomenon known as "Summer Folk."

become so energy conscious, wondered aloud to a Vermont farmer about what he should do with his garbage. The enterprising farmer promptly sold him a pig for fifteen dollars. When the summer was over, this same New Jersey man again sought advice from the farmer as to what he should do with the aforementioned pig, as he was returning to the city for the winter. Quite quickly, our farmer replied that he would be glad to take it off his hands for ten dollars, seeing as how the New Jersey man had had use of the pig all summer.

SUMMER IN VERMONT

HAY AS A TOURIST ATTRACTION

I'll bet it has been little tricks like this, plus the utterly ridiculous prices that have been charged for property, that have endeared us to them so much. Regardless of the reason, we surely must be fast friends, 'cause they just keep on coming, more and more each year.

Now, in some sort of balance or moderation, we welcome these people, and not only for their company, but also for the benefits to us they bring with them. The first of these is the property taxes they pay on the back-farms, and summer homes, and cottages they have built or bought here. And for many a tax-poor town they have surely been a lifesaver. The next benefit is their need for goods and services while they are here. They have the effect of a double shot on many local and area merchants and service workers, thereby making it possible for them to continue in business in their particular locations. So as not to become a criminal in the eyes of my peers, I guess I ought to cut out this flattery of summer neighbors and shut this story right down.

"Regardless of the reason, we surely must be fast friends, 'cause they just keep on coming, more and more each year."

PROFESSOR DAVID K. SMITH

In the 1960s and 1970s, David Smith was another avid collector, not of mushrooms, or flowers, or birds, but of humor.

From David Smith's perspective, 96 percent of Middlebury College students are deprived. They are not native Vermonters.

But Smith believes that this handicap, while total, need not be fatal. As a teacher—professor of economics at Middlebury for twenty-seven years—the fifty-six-year-old Pittsford native feels obligated to enlighten these benighted souls.

Every three years, therefore, Smith dons the baggy trousers, rubber boots, flannel shirt, and wool cap of the stereo-typical Vermont farmer, and gives a lecture on "The native Vermonter and his sense of humor."

The speech originated in his economics classes, where he began telling Vermont jokes to regain the students' flagging attention. About ten years ago, he surveyed wider pastures. "Winter term was filled with some pretty heavy lectures on things like 17th century poetry and thermodynamics. I asked the administration if I could talk about Vermont humor, and they agreed."

Smith made no pretense of being a Vermont humor scholar. "That honor goes to Allen Foley (retired Dartmouth professor and member of the Vermont Legislature). But then, Foley came from Massachusetts!"

Smith became famous enough to take his talk on the road around Vermont, where the Vermont Association of Town Clerks was most appreciative. A group of out-of-towners who heard him speak at a posh resort were clueless.

Smith grew up in the Pittsford-Proctor area. His voice, he admits, has lost some of its pure Vermont timbre, through "eight years of adulteration by Harvard and the US Army."

But the pace, precision, and acute articulation of each syllable probably sounded genuine to the outlanders.

"To understand Vermont humor, you have to understand something about life in small towns. In Pittsford, we didn't have a drugstore or a movie house. And Brandon was a big-deal city. Not much happened and mostly I remember not remembering much of anything. One of the biggest things to do was to go down to Clark's bakery and buy a jelly doughnut and sit down on the corner step with a copy of *True Love* magazine."

To Smith, the essential humor consists of "fairly unique insights into very simple situations." An example: "In Pittsford there was a very large lady married to a very small man. One day, a neighbor happened to walk past the couple's house and saw the woman shaking out the bedding. Being a helpful sort, he called out, 'Hey, Mable, if you're looking for John, he's out to the barn.'

Well, I'm damned if I'll go down there for just a Nickel.

A farmer and his Flatlander friend found themselves in the same two-hole outhouse. As the farmer rose from his seat, a nickel fell out of his pocket. Quick as a wink, he pulled out his wallet, plucked out a five-dollar bill, and threw it into the hole after the nickel.

'What are you doing!?' said the flabbergasted Flatlander. 'Well, I'm damned if I'll go down there for just a nickel!'"

David Smith finished his "lecture" by telling of a bakery in Middlebury which served coffee and pastries, and had a few tables where one could sit and chat.

"One day, a fellow named Johnny Kenworthy came in, ordered a cup of coffee and a doughnut, and went to sit down. Minutes later, he was back at the counter and asked to exchange his doughnut for two cookies. 'Sure,' said the baker.

In due course, he finished his coffee and cookies. On his way out, he left a dime by the cash register.

'But, John,' said the baker, 'you paid for the coffee but not the cookies.'

'I gave you a doughnut for those cookies,' John huffed.

'But you didn't pay for the doughnut,' replied the now-exasperated baker.

'Didn't EAT the doughnut!' said John, and walked proudly out the door.[29]

DON NOTCHES THE GUNWALE

Senator Mark MacDonald and Don Hooper were fishing up at the Floating Bridge in Brookfield the other evening. It was just after "ice-out" in late April. As ill-timing would have it, just as serious dusk descended on us, Mark tucked into a mother lode of hungry trout. He was sitting in the front seat of our rental skiff, and pulling in some beauts, rapid-fire, off the gunwale on the starboard bow.

But, unfortunately, we both had an obligation that couldn't be postponed. We were expected at the East Bethel Grange supper where we were "the Program." Annually, in front of an audience of at least a dozen skeptics, we made up the panel of local "electeds" who were expected to account for what this year's

General Assembly did or didn't accomplish. Absence was not an option.

Always insecure about being re-elected in a competitive district, I said, "Marko, we gotta scoot. Can't be late to the Grange. But here's a brilliant idea. Why not take out your jackknife and notch the gunwale exactly where you're catching all these fish? Tomorrow we can come back and catch the rest of them."

But MacDonald, being a state senator, was always smarter than a lowly and limited House member. As I started to row us back to the dock, Marko proclaimed, "That might not work. What if they give us a different boat tomorrow?"

By the time I'd tell the story that night at the Grange, I'd have embellished it a tad. I warn't no Mark Twain, but maybe three attendees would crack a smile over the self-deprecation; that was considered success on the hustings.

> **By the time I'd tell the story that night at the Grange, I'd have embellished it a tad.**

IRON LOGIC

When the Vermont State Hospital, in Waterbury, Vermont, still had patients who had degrees of freedom, a visitor from New York came to see friends who lived along Main Street in Waterbury Village. A real Nosey Parker, this woman ("such a busy-body she'd want to teach a dog to scratch"). For several days, this woman watched an earnest gentleman walking up and down the street several times a day, in animated conversation with himself.

Finally, she could stand it no longer. She strode down the stairs and planted herself in front of the gentleman, so he had to stop.

"Excuse me, sir," she opened politely, "but I've been watching you talking to yourself as if there were no tomorrow. Why?"

"That's easy, ma'am. For one thing, I want to be with someone who has something to say, and for another, I like to go walking with a good listener."

✦

WILL E. SOAKUM, ESQ.,
ATTORNEY-AT-BAY
FOR WHIPLASH,
SAPSUCKER +
STONEBLEED
FILES A CITIZEN SUIT.

Q: Are you a lawyer?

A: Yes.

Q: What do you charge?

A: Four hundred dollars for four questions.

Q: That's pretty expensive, isn't it?

A: Yup. What's your fourth question?

Hey, Mr. Farmer, Dontcha think it would save time if you just shook the tree and let the pig eat the apples off the ground.

"Ah, p'haps, But, really, what's time to a pig?"

✦

I really shouldn't have done this, but bear with me, I'm eighty-four years old and terrified of getting COVID–19. So, I'm doing all kinds of social distancing things I've never done before. Today, I was in my car, in a long queue at The Village Scoop creemee stand in Colchester. The young woman behind me, who had New York plates, got exasperated with my elderly confusion as I tried to decide between Tasty Turtle, Cheery Blossom, Cookies and Cream, and Peppermint Stick. She leaned on her horn and mouthed something I presumed to be impolite, because she was in a hurry and I was taking too long to order.

So, when I got to the first window, I paid for her order along with my own. The cashier must have told her what I'd done, because as we crept forward, the impatient New Yorker leaned out her window and mouthed a big, sheepish "Thank You," clearly embarrassed that I'd repaid her rudeness with a kindness.

When I got to the pick-up window, I showed both receipts and accepted both orders of food. How guilty do I feel, now that Ms. Getamoveon had to go all the way back to the end of the line and start over? Not so much.

Moral? Be nice.

Preferring both belt and suspenders, Maude + Jethro considered themselves "conservative."

CHAPTER 4

Came to Stay

In the 1980s, Vermont was changing, and its humor had to change as well. Fortunately, that's when UVM political science professor Frank Bryan and I stepped in. Inspired by a new national book, *Real Men Don't Eat Quiche,* we came up with our own satire about Vermont: *Real Vermonters Don't Milk Goats.* Its exquisite timing made the book a perfect documentation of the shift in Vermont's social landscape to dominance by the immigrant "Flatlanders."

We found the right tone, which sliced suspenders but still left the pants on.

✦

We celebrated real people and poked fun at real politicians. There were even rivalries within the state: Northern Vermont residents kidded Southern Vermonters as living in the "Banana Belt," while the rest of Vermont joked that residents of rich and prosperous Chittenden County were happy because they lived "so close to Vermont."

REAL VERMONTERS DON'T WEAR L.L. BEAN BOOTS

It gets more and more difficult to tell a Real Vermonter from a Flatlander. This is because many Flatlanders do their best to look like Real Vermonters. Here are some hints that might help:

Real Vermonters don't wear hiking boots in town, headbands on the street, or running shoes when they walk. You will never see a Real Vermonter in leather pants. Real Vermonters get dressed up for church, weddings, funerals, and graduations. Real Vermonters don't have undershirts with writing on them. Anyone seen at Town Meeting in Levi's is not a Real Vermonter. Real Vermonters never have fur inside their gloves.

They never wear cowboy hats or string ties. No one seen under an umbrella is ever a Real Vermonter. Most of all, Real Vermonters never, ever try to look like Real Vermonters.

Vermont bumper sticker: "Gut deer?"

LIFE

- An active solar system is a clothesline.
- A Real Vermonter's bed doesn't ebb and flow.
- Real Vermont pets don't get haircuts.
- No Real Vermont house has barn boards inside.
- No Real Vermont house is known by the name of its current owners.
- A Real Vermont farmer is someone who gets up in town meeting and identifies himself as a farmer, and no one laughs!

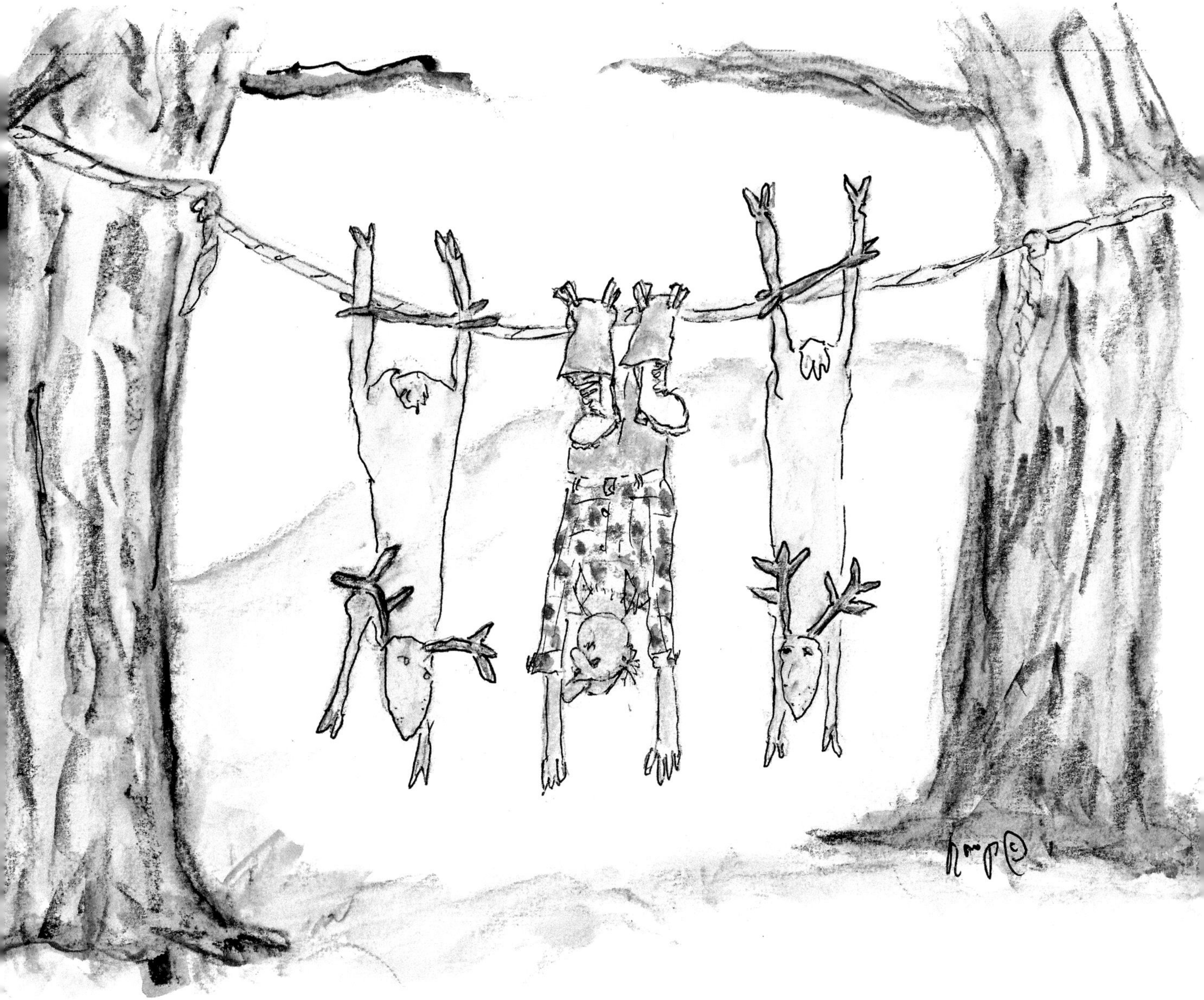

HOW DO YOU KNOW WHEN REAL VERMONTERS LIKE YOU?

Only Flatlanders know the glow that comes when they discover that a Real Vermonter likes them. Here are a few signs that such bliss may be near:

- They invite you in through the kitchen door.
- They don't call you before they come to visit.
- They don't ask you if you'd rather have decaf coffee.
- They don't remind you to put on your snow tires.
- They don't come to visit during deer season, on the first day of trout season, any Sunday afternoon in October, or until after the driveway dries up in April.
- They don't offer you extra vegetables from their gardens.
- When they see you, they don't say any of the following: "How's the family?" or "We've got to get together sometime when things settle down a bit" or "How's by you?"
- They don't call to tell you to cover the tomatoes.
- They don't offer to help unless you need it.

Vermont child-rearing adage: "If you plant corn, you get corn."

THINGS REAL VERMONTERS ARE BORN WITH

- Patience.
- A sense of where "north" is.
- An inclination to say "no."
- The ability to drive in the snow.
- One leg shorter than the other.
- A talent for telling time without a watch.

- One thousand different ways to indicate the affirmative.
- Knowledge about angles and leverage.
- A taste for boiled greens of any kind.
- An ability to tell New Hampshire from Vermont.
- A dexterity for milking cows blindfolded.
- No fear of the truth.

FENCE PLIERS AND JUMPER CABLES *(Your Vermont Toolkit)*

Vermonters pride themselves on their ability to "make do" with as little as possible. That is why duct tape sells so well. It also explains Bag Balm and bailing twine. Nevertheless, from time to time you may have to do some repair work in Vermont. Here are some other tools to have handy, as well:

- A fishing pole.
- A copy of *Robert's Rules of Order*.
- The capacity to grin and bear it.
- Hope.
- Needle-nosed pliers.
- Directions back to New Jersey.
- Tolerance.
- A 12-gauge shotgun.
- Bug repellent.
- A copy of the *Vermont Constitution*.
- The willingness to live and let live.
- A chainsaw file.
- A second source of income.

- Mittens.
- Jumper cables.
- Boots in the trunk.
- A bright orange hat.
- A plumber's helper.

✦

Governor Madeleine Kunin's older brother, Edgar May, earned his perch as one of the Vermont legislature's genuine, certifiable "characters." After hustling his way into the state senate from Windsor County, "Egger" waxed nostalgic over what he'd left behind by "trading up" from his former House seat representing Springfield.

"Why, in the House, I could give a stem-winder and turn forty votes. In the Senate, their minds are all made up before the bill's even been drafted!"

"Hey, you see what hippie Plainfield Rep. Peter Youngbaer's sponsoring? A bill to make the fiddlehead fern the Vermont State Vegetable! Those crunchy granolas from Plainfield just can't resist *Stalking the Wild Asparagus*. Next, they'll want to declare the jumper cable the Vermont State Tool."

✦

Even if a Flatlander's children have the good fortune to be born in Vermont, they will be reminded of their irrevocable Flatlander status when their Vermont neighbor cites the adage: "when a cat has kittens in the oven, we don't call 'em 'muffins.'"

QUESTIONS A REAL VERMONTER WOULD NEVER ASK

Your car is stuck in a snow bank. It's zero degrees outside and the wind is howling. Just as your hope begins to fade, up drives a shiny Bronco or Renegade. The driver jumps out to help.

- "Boy, it's too cold to be stuck out here," you say.
- "It sure is," says the other driver. "I wonder what the wind-chill factor is?"

Bingo! You know it's a Flatlander. If you listen carefully, you can hear other Flatlanders betray their origins by the questions they ask.

Here are some more:

- What's your sign?
- How deep do they plant them?
- Where does the sap come from?
- Where's a good place to picnic around here?
- Have you read *Real Vermonters Don't Milk Goats?*
- Where can I buy the *New York Times*?
- What's the "R" factor?
- How many BTUs does it generate?
- How big do the horns have to be?
- Where were you born?
- Do you have a view of the mountains?

REAL VERMONTERS DON'T SAY "LET'S SEE HOW THIS SUGARS OFF"

✦

HOLLYWOOD INVADES VERMONT

For eight seasons, through the 1980s, the rest of the country (and some Vermonters) watched Hollywood's take on Vermont through CBS's sitcom, *The Bob Newhart Show*. The show, stocked with odd animals and odd people, details the misadventures of a New York writer, named Dick (Newhart), who buys and runs an inn in rural East Middlebury, Vermont, with his wife, Joanna (the now-late Mary Frann).

Newhart always said he wanted to end the series early, because he'd seen "too many shows that had overstayed their welcome." So, for the final episode, a Japanese tycoon buys up the whole town to turn it into a golf resort. Other than Dick and Joanna, everyone takes buyouts and moves away, even the hapless local Larry and his seemingly mute brothers, named Darryl and Darryl. For eight seasons, the pair carried Vermont taciturnity to its local extreme. They said not a word, until a moment in the finale when their three wives were chattering on and they turned and in unison yelled, "QUIET!" At which the nonplussed Newhart says, "Your brothers can speak?"

Newhart always said he wanted to end the series early, because he'd seen "too many shows that had overstayed their welcome."

TALKIN' CHUCK

by Stephen Morris

Say you're on a golf course and you hear someone yell Foah!—you'd better hit the dirt—a Vermonter with three clubs (all carried under his arm) has just teed off.

In native Chuckese, the number nine is pronounced noyne, to rhyme with groin. The number five is pronounced foyve, to rhyme with loyve, as in loyve bait. Here are a few terms and their definitions, so you will not be out of place at Thunder Road or the beer hall at the Tunbridge World's Fair.

When Mother not happy. Nobody Happy.

Some: This all-purpose word is perhaps the most important in all Chuckdom, as it extends any other descriptive adjective. Hard to explain, but easy to demonstrate: "Some cold today." "That dress was some expensive."

Don't you know? (Sounds like Dontchuno?): A phrase without meaning, used gratuitously in conversation. Appropriate at the end of a sentence or fragment thereof. Often used in conjunction with some. Example: "Some cold today, dontchuno?"

Mother: One's wife, girlfriend, or significant other (now there is a Flatlander term!), as in "Mother gets some peeved when I drink too many beers, dontchuno!" Or, "That was one mother of a wind last night!"

Jeezum Crow (locally, boi jeezum, boi the jeezum, or boi the jumpin' jeezum.): A North Country epithet with religious implications. Just stay out of the way of anyone who gets to the jumpin' jeezum stage, especially if he is either drunk or has a gun.

Creemee: A soft, iced-milk confection dispensed at roadside stands and quick-stops in the North. Served in several flavors, but any flavor beyond maple is superfluous. Ben & Jerry's, with their White Russian Double Cheesecake Chocolate Cherry Chunk, will never reach this audience.

Dubblewoid: A trailer, or prefabricated home, double the normal sixteen-foot width, for many the fulfillment of a lifelong dream. Spelled "doublewide." Often seen on interstate highways with accompanying signage: WOID LOAD.

Noice spread: An array of food at a social gathering, including cheese cubes (Velveeta®), Ritz® crackers, decorated Spam®, and quart bottles of Genesee® beer. "Noice Spread" is a useful phrase to mutter repeatedly at a potluck dinner.

Doodlebug: An off-road vehicle, specifically for hauling wood, often a testament to mechanical genius. Once the forward gears are stripped, one turns the seat around, and reverse becomes forward.[30]

> **"Boi the jeezum, Mother were some wickid frosty when I dickered away the dubblewoid for a doodlebug that don't run good."**

In our book, *The Vermont Owner's Manual*, Frank Bryan and I added to Morris's list.

Wicked: An adjective used to denote the extreme. As in, "Buster is a *wicked* big bull." Or, "The belle of the prom could be *wicked* pretty." And a February morning, "*wicked* cold." Coherent hyperbole would be "*Jumpin Jeezum,* it was wicked hot, *dontchuno!*"

Dickerin': To negotiate. Often used in advertisements to indicate a price is not "firm." As in, "For sale: A *dubblewoid* trailer. *Wicked* good for snow-machines. $750. Will *dicker.* (Or swap for a *doodlebug.*)"

Contrary to their name, mobile homes are not mobile, and they cannot be bartered for a "runs good" doodlebug.

SPEED IS NOT OF THE ESSENCE

Clem Eldridge, a Vermont carpenter, was winterizing a saggy porch on an old cape for a down-country baron who intended spending more of his leisure skiing in Vermont. Watching Clem dub with fussy finish work for a couple of days, the Flatlander bluntly confronted the carpenter. "I wonder if you could pick up the pace a little." Un-fazed, Clem responded, "Oh, I don't think I can do that, Mr. Higglebotham. Can't really go faster, but I can go a whole lot slower."

We celebrated real people and poked fun at real politicians.

CHAPTER 5

Doing the People's Business…
Sometimes

When people seek the public's eye and vote, when they strive to get in your face and in your head, they risk a certain embarrassment. They might present themselves as infallible, but they are wrong. All kinds of traps and snares lay in wait, many self-set.

It was while serving in the Vermont House that I began mining the rich ore of Vermont's political humor. In my third term, I was appointed to the Education Committee, but my bigger work was to serve as vice-chair of the Vermont Bicentennial Commission, which provided more opportunities to ride around the state. Frank Bryan, my co-author for two other books, suggested that a zoo full of odd creatures, harmless pretention, and bumbling egotism begged for a third book.

Ultimately, we packaged these stories (and others) in a book called *Out of Order*. To illustrate the book, we hired fellow representative Don Hooper, a lively, lifelong amateur cartoonist. The modest story line involved two janitors collecting "stories" from desks and waste baskets, committee tables, and hallways. They then hid these "unofficial State House archives" in a strongbox in the basement men's room. A number of the following stories are from that collection.

Many years ago, it was fairly common practice in Vermont for funerals to be conducted without benefit of clergy, particularly in the most rural areas. The service would consist of appropriate music and reading of the scripture by some volunteer. Following which, upon invitation from the mortician, a few friends would relate an incident involving the deceased, or deliver short words of eulogy.

On one such occasion a funeral was taking place in a back-road section of Calais. After the music and the reading of scripture, the mortician asked, "Would anyone like to say a few words on behalf of the deceased?"

A long, embarrassed silence ensued. Finally, a gentleman in a back seat stood and said, "If no one else cares to talk on behalf of the deceased, I would like to take this opportunity say a few words on behalf of the Republican Party."[31]

A LONG TIME AGO

Election officials were counting ballots in an Orange County town, forty or fifty years ago. After piling up a stack of Republican ballots three inches high, the counters found a Democratic vote. They counted another pile of Republican votes, when a second Democratic ballot surfaced.

"Humpf!" exclaimed one election commissioner. "That S.O.B. must have voted twice!"

EATING HUMBLE PIE

Democrat Frank Branon ran for governor in 1954, at a time when Democrats were as rare as hens' teeth. There hadn't been a Democratic candidate for governor in almost a hundred years.

But Branon was a game campaigner, and traveled the state tirelessly. One night, in mid-October, he and his wife found themselves at a church supper in Fairfax. Branon bolted his food, then took the "stage" to make his appeal to a sober and somber group of diners. Meanwhile, his wife settled in with a group of women, toward the back of the hall.

Branon spoke well, even eliciting a smile or two from the audience. When he finished, his wife thought the moment was ripe for her own appeal. She leaned across the table and whispered to the woman who had been the most animated during the speech.

"Excuse me, but I'd sure appreciate it if you could support my husband in the election."

"Oh, no! I'm so sorry," said the woman. "We can't do that. We've been Vermonters all our lives!"

Lived in Vermont all yer life, Cyrus?

Not yet.

RIGHT ON THE MONEY

In January 1971, Representative Walter "Peanut" Kennedy (R-Chelsea) was running for Speaker of the House of Representatives. Kennedy was confident he would win, but skepticism was rife in the State House press corps.

"How many votes will you get, Peanut?" they asked.

"Ninety-two!" he said to surprised reporters. And, come the election, he got exactly those ninety-two.

"How did you figure that?" they asked.

"Well, first I counted the Republicans who said they would vote for me. Then I counted the Democrats who I thought would vote for me. And I didn't ask for any commitments.

"Then I took away the ones who had said they would vote for me, but I knew wouldn't. I subtracted ten percent for erosion, and that's how I arrived at ninety-two."

WORDS, WORDS, WORDS

In 1982, one William J. Leahy (no relation of US Senator Patrick J. Leahy) ran for Sheriff of Franklin County. His campaign posters promised "Compassion, Empathy, and Rhetoric."[32] Even some of his supporters scratched their heads at the last word. Did Leahy know the English language?

"Of course," he replied. "Rhetoric means the art of effective communications. I used the word deliberately, so people would have a reason to ask me about it, and I could explain why I'm running."

Apparently, not enough people were intrigued or curious about his explanation, for, on Election Day, he lost.

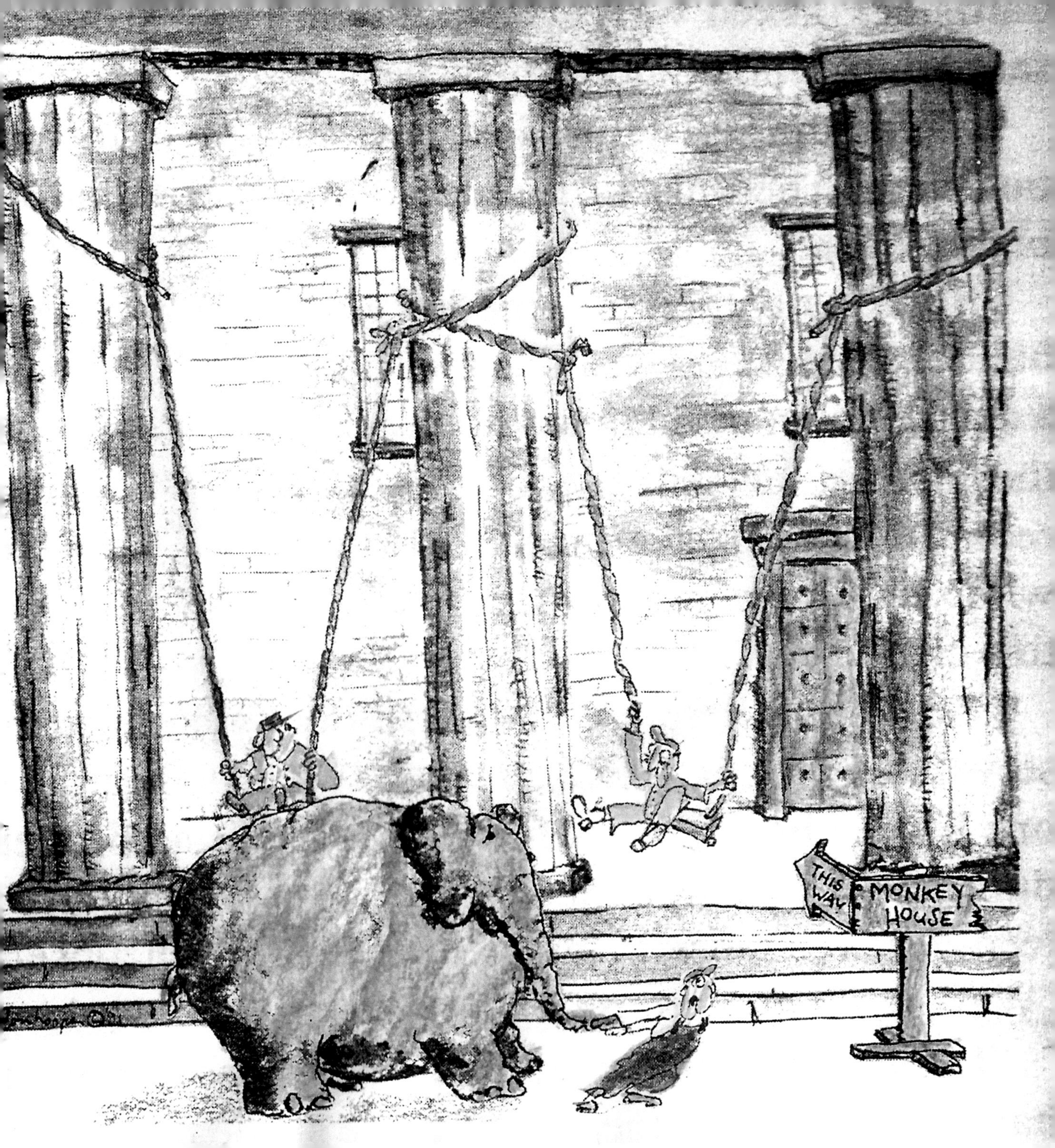
THIS WAY
MONKEY HOUSE

KING REID

Reid Lefevre (R-Manchester) served in the House and Senate for over twenty years. He was a big man who looked like H. L. Mencken, and he revered the English language in the same way. There was a bit of P.T. Barnum in him, as well, for he owned a circus which traveled around the East when the legislature was not in session. In 1947, "King Reid" brought the circus to the State House, and put up a sign over one door: "This way to the Monkey House."

Like Mencken, he, too, had a cutting wit. Once, during a debate about whether to dock members' pay when they had unexcused absences, he killed the bill with a single remark: "Mr. Speaker, there are members of the House who serve most generously when they are absent from this chamber!"

St. Patrick drives the snakes out
of the Northeast Kingdom.

A DEATHBED CONVERSION

Father John Mahoney and his brother-in-law attorney (later, federal judge), Bernard Leddy, were rabid Democrats. During World War II, Mahoney went with the National Guard to the South Pacific. When the troop ship *Coolidge* struck a mine and was sunk in 1942, Mahoney found himself floating in the sea.[33] He promised St. Jude to build a church in his honor if he survived. After the war, he fulfilled that promise with a church in Hinesburg.

During his ministry there, he was called to give last rites to a dying man who lived in the hills northeast of the village. As Mahoney was finishing the anointing, a neighbor stopped to visit. Seeing a priest, the visitor was amazed. "I never knew he was a Catholic. He's been a Republican all his life!"

Putting the stole and holy oil back into their travel cases, Mahoney spoke with the satisfaction of having brought a sinner to salvation just in the nick of time. "Well, he's a Democrat now!"

"Some folks called him the Vermont Yogi Berra."

GILLYISMS

Politicians talk a lot. They're expected to have an answer for everything. Often, in their rush to persuade, they fall back on clichés or hackneyed phrases. But sometimes they creatively combine, inadvertently, these images into new and arresting forms.

Few members of the Vermont legislature ever sowed such a bumper crop as did Senator Gilbert Godnick (D-Rutland). His malapropisms were so numerous and adroit, some folks called him the Vermont Yogi Berra. Here is a Whitman's Sampler of Gilly's confections:

- "The squeaky wheel gets the ointment."
- "Bed and breakfast places are nothing more than sleep and eat places."
- "The first law of science is you've got to take care of yourself."
- "There's always one rotten egg in every barrel of apples."
- "Foliage and skiism are just parts of tourism."
- "You three guys make a pair!"
- "The polls don't count. What counts is when the voters go behind the iron curtain."
- "You can lead a horse to water, but you can't look him in the eye."
- "That's a horse of a different ballgame."
- "We'll burn that bridge when we get to it."
- "This bill will be greeted in Rutland like a ham sandwich at a Bar Mitzvah."

This is a horse of a whole new ballgame.

KISSINGER AND FOREIGN POLICY

In the summer of 1976, economist John Kenneth Galbraith hosted a convocation of government leaders and academics at his summer home in Townshend. Among the guests was Secretary of State Henry Kissinger.

Before and during the gathering, the Secret Service had its work cut out. These unsmiling, wary men had rarely needed to protect public figures in the woods. So, they recruited some local Windham County deputies to help on the perimeter, and to chauffeur some of the guests.

One Sunday, as Kissinger was being driven to the Four Columns Restaurant for lunch, he was met by an aide with the day's cables of world events.

As Kissinger leafed through the telegrams, he muttered to himself, "Ach, more shooting in Lebanon!"

"Oh, don't worry Mr. Secretary," interjected an eager deputy who'd become quite comfortable with Kissinger throughout his assignment. "That's over in New Hampshire. It's out of our jurisdiction."

MAKING WITNESSES ILL AT EASE

Tired of witnesses who either over-qualified their statements or failed to answer direct questions, three members of the House Ways and Means Committee, Representatives Barbara Grimes, Don Hooper, and Mark MacDonald, devised and printed a Witness Evaluation List, and hung it in the committee room. Witnesses could not fail to read its Dantesque gradations as they faced chairman Oreste Valsangiacomo and his fellow committee members. The list graded witness credibility thus:

10. Scrupulously honest
9. Decently accurate
8. An inadvertent omission
7. Hmmm, a slip here or there
6. Disrespectful of the facts
5. Slight of mouth
4. Verisimilitudinous is too kind
3. Prevaricates abundantly
2. A sleazy rip-off
1. The dog ate my testimony

O TEMPORE O MORES

In the spring of 1986, there came to the House floor, via the Health and Welfare Committee, a senate bill "relating to the licensing of persons who perform manicures and facials."

Representative Eugene Godt (D-Brookline) was entrusted to report (explain) the bill on the House floor.

Almost every bill introduced in either house includes a few definitions of words that relate to the proposed legislation. Thus, Godt began his reporting of the bill with the definition of *esthetics*.

"Mr. Speaker, esthetics means massaging, cleansing, stimulating, exercising, beautifying, or otherwise working on the scalp, face, neck, arms, bust, or upper part of the body by the use of any manner of cosmetic preparations, antiseptics, tonics, lotions, or creams."

Godt paused. "Now, Mr. Speaker, those are the words of an inspired poet or a word processor in heat!"

When the laughter around the House died down, Godt sheepishly remarked, "Mr. Speaker, I think I have lost my place!"

"Member from Brookline, I thought you had found it," observed Speaker Ralph Wright.

"Whew," said Godt, "I *have* had two sinking feelings and a hot flash, just standing here!"

A VERMONTER IN THE UNITED NATIONS

Believe it or not, the United States chose, as its first ambassador to the
United Nations, a Yankee from Vermont—the only New England state
without a coastline. When former mayor of St. Albans and US Senator
Warren Austin stepped to the podium to deliver his nation's maiden address
to the planet, one crisis center was then, as it is now, the Middle East. Austin
approached the subject in true Vermont style—head-on. He closed his
speech to the UN General Assembly with the ringing plea: "It is time for
the Arabs and the Jews to learn to cooperate in true Christian fashion."

To add kindness to his anarchy, Norbert served bacon to his Muslim and Jewish customers alike.

THE GREAT SEAT BELT DEBATE

In 1986, a bill to require the wearing of seat belts came before the full Vermont House of Representatives. Over the course of two days, depending on their perspective, members debated this "sensible contribution to public safety and welfare" or "this further government meddling in the rights of free citizens."

In lieu of seat belts, fire trucks chose Velcro.

   As the debate proceeded, opponents and supporters sought to amend the bill, either to make it more acceptable or to make it more ridiculous and cumbersome. Exemptions were suggested for garbage truck drivers, emergency medical personnel, delivery workers, even volunteer firefighters. Over this last exemption, much debate ensued, though the bill called for seat belt use only if the belts were built into the vehicle, a feature absent from fire trucks.

   Taking a break in the lobby, Representative Ann Harroun (D-Essex) overheard one wag's solution for the firefighters' dilemma: "Why don't they just put a big strip of Velcro around the fire trucks and add the same to the fighters' coats? That will allow them to jump on and off more safely."

   She returned to the floor just in time to hear a final exemption offered by Representative Keith Wallace (R-Waterbury): "Mr. Speaker, my proposal is to exempt all legislators, who are already equipped with airbags!"

SPREAD FRED

In 1998, Vermont filmmaker John O'Brien decided that art should imitate life. O'Brien had recently finished a film called *Man with a Plan,* about an ill-educated, tottering, retired dairy farmer who runs for US Congress as Vermont's sole representative.

As a publicity boost for the film, O'Brien persuaded his real-life neighbor-farmer-actor, Fred Tuttle of Tunbridge, to run for actual office, and enter the state's Republican primary to take on Vermont's incumbent Senator-for-Life, Patrick J. Leahy.

As a hometown, homespun actor, Tuttle had already become famous through *Man with a Plan,* watering Vermont's fields with freshets, if not torrents, of humor and the self-evident. In the 1996 general election, Tunbridge's 601 voters gave Mr. Tuttle five write-in votes for United States Representative, six for governor, one for lieutenant governor, three for state treasurer, two for secretary of state, one for attorney general, two for state senator, two for state representative, and a whopping fourteen for high bailiff —always an enigmatic office for both Real Vermonters and those from away.

For this actual race, in 1998, Tuttle was game, but promised never to be seated if he won. But, first, he needed to win the primary.

The Republican establishment groused that Tuttle was just a stalking horse for Democratic filmmaker, O'Brien.

As the campaign progressed, with humor and creativity, Tuttle earned his underdog role of hapless yokel and incorrigible bygone-era Vermont dairy farmer. His smug, wealthy carpetbagger opponent, Jim McMullen from Massachusetts, became known as "McMillion$," thus securing the David vs. Goliath contest in Vermonters' imaginations. Tuttle pressed McMullen to debate, but the Republican repeatedly refused. By August, however, public pressure and Tuttle's increasing folk-hero popularity forced McMullen to agree to a daytime debate on Vermont Public Radio.

Midway through the debate, the two were permitted to quiz each other. Tuttle handed his opponent a short list of Vermont towns with

When farmer Tuttle deadpanned, in his trademark Tunbridge accent, "What's a teddah?" McMullen was toast.

uniquely Vermont pronunciations. For the first, McMullen whiffed on the French-seeming "Calais."

Next, Tuttle inquired, "How many teats does a Holstein have?" Flummoxed, McMullen picked an improbable number, other than four.

When farmer Tuttle deadpanned, in his trademark Tunbridge accent, "What's a teddah?" McMullen was toast.[34]

Tuttle won the primary with 54 percent of the vote. He then promptly endorsed Leahy, and campaigned with him in the general election. In that vote, he still got 22 percent, leaving pundits to ponder if those votes were really for him or just those of disgruntled Republicans voting "Anybody But Leahy."

After the race, filmmaker O'Brien observed, "Fred enjoyed being famous. If anyone didn't know who Fred Tuttle was, he was incredulous."

WHERE THE AFFLUENT MEET THE EFFLUENT

In 1986, the Vermont legislature was in the throes of a pitched battle over the fate of its headwaters. The pristine mountain streams that originated high in the Green Mountains, where the ski areas were expanding, became endangered when developers proposed using "treated sewage" to make skiable snow. Environmentalists objected, saying the spring snowmelt would shock the headwaters with pollution. The enviros vs. ski corporations war became known as "Kunin versus Killington." In that larger war for clean water, two legislative skirmishers were Rep. Don Chioffi (D-Rutland Town) and Bill Mares (D- Burlington) who distributed a brown and white bumper sticker labeled: "KILLINGTON—Where the Affluent meet the Effluent."

DOYLE POLL

Washington County State Senator William "Bill" Doyle stayed elected for an incredible forty-eight years. Famously, Bill administered the "Doyle Poll" each Town Meeting Day, in which he'd compose a dozen questions on Vermont's issues-of-the-day. Sometimes he'd bias the answers to reflect his hoped-for outcomes. Here's a slightly hyperbolic example:

> "Should the drinking age be raised to thirty-two?"
> "The Gubernatorial term ought to be raised to ten years, dontchya think?"

Doyle persuaded legislators to carry his "Doyle Poll" to every town in their districts, and then collect the completed surveys. The survey results, which Senator Doyle would announce with great fanfare, had not a scintilla of statistical science or credibility, but they always made it into the *Times Argus*. The Doyle Poll made the Dean of the Vermont Senate a household name throughout the state. It also made Bill the object of some playful derision. Cartoons such as this one were periodically posted on the door of his Senate Government Operations Committee Room.

Doyle Pole

CHASING THE VOTERS

In 1986, two-term State Representative Howard Dean (D-Burlington) launched his campaign for lieutenant governor. In many local communities, he asked for help from fellow legislators. One of them was Mark MacDonald (D-Williamstown), who recalled, "I had agreed to take Howard around Williamstown to meet some farmers. We drove some of the backroads and finally stopped at one farm where we could see this guy way out in the field tedding hay. Howard wanted to go meet him. So we got out of the car and started walking across the field. About halfway there, I realized this farmer was a woman.

"Then, as we got closer, I could see her reaching behind her to pull out some cloth. Damned if she wasn't shirtless. I knelt down to tie my shoe.

"I hollered to Howard, but he was too intent on jumping windrows and getting to this voter. I could see the tractor laying down the crookedest windrow you ever saw, as the woman tried to drive and put her shirt on at the same time.

"When Howard got about twenty feet from her, he looked up, and by that time she still had only a couple of buttons done. He stopped in his tracks and turned around. She stopped the tractor and finished buttoning her shirt. Howard was blushing, but he still managed to make his campaign pitch."

BERNIE AND BERNIE

by Julie Davis

Bernie Sanders appointed me City Constable in his second term as Mayor of the City of Burlington. During that time, our family dog was also named Bernie, and lived with my parents in South Burlington. Bernie was a husky-Labrador mix with an anxious temperament, so terrified of thunder, he once jumped through a screen door into the house with his collar still hitched to the outside run.

BRED TO BARK

One stormy Sunday, my parents went out of town and I was to go over to the house to sedate him in the event a storm came through. Feeling a bit run down, I decided to take a nap before heading over. When I woke up, I was in a groggy state of mind, and decided to ask my brother David to check on Bernie, so I wouldn't have to go to the house.

My brother had recently moved, and had a new number. I was fortunate to find it handy, on a piece of paper on the table.

When David answered, I said, "Hi David, this is Julie—I just woke up and I'm exhausted. Bernie is at the house and needs someone to go over to sedate him. Can you do that for me?"

Bernie is at the house and needs someone to go over to sedate him. Can you do that for me?

There was a long pause at the other end of the phone, so I said, "You know how he is about thunderstorms, right?"

Again, there was a long pause, not at all characteristic of my brother. "David?" I said.

"Yeah," said David.

Again, this was not a characteristic response, so I said, "David Davis?"

He said, "No, this is David Weinstein!"

At that time, I was working closely with David Weinstein on campaign matters, and had confused the numbers. We both had a good laugh at the thought of Bernie hunkered down on Catherine Street, waiting for someone to come and sedate him due to a thunderstorm.

MARK TWAIN USED TO SAY:
"GET YER FACTS FIRST,
THEN YOU CAN DISTORT 'EM AS YOU PLEASE."

CHAPTER 6

A Yard Sale of Vermont Humorists

These compositions, like all good humor, are weeds in the DMZ between truth and falsehood, a veritable "Vermont's Got Talent" of roses, nettles, sweet corn, and poison ivy.

THE TIMEKEEPER
by William Boardman

[The Timekeeper is alone on stage.]

Well, I've been timekeeper here 'bout as long as I can remember. Maybe as long as there's memory. Who's to say for sure?

Now, being timekeeper ain't such a bad job, you know—most of the time's no trouble at all. Oh, I reckon the hours get a little long sometimes, and their tails get dangerous—but they're not vicious. Nope, not at all like the split seconds. You got to be so dang careful with the split seconds! Else they get under your nails and bite like the very devil. Fussy eaters, too.

Of course, the easiest to handle are the years. Great lumbering beasts, why the years could break you in half if they wanted to. Luckily, they don't want—easy, big fella!—least not usually. Most folks don't seem to realize it, but your years don't actually chew anything. They just sort of suck on their food. Till it dissolves.

Not like the decades, at all! Their sharp little teeth can tear most anything to shreds. You got to be careful, you'll lose an arm to the decades, easy. Maybe worse.

And the centuries! Why, the centuries, they just swallow you whole if you give 'em a chance—or even if you don't. Good thing there's only a few of them.

Now, most folks seem to prefer the minutes best, 'cause they're so playful, I guess. See that pair, tumbling over there in the corner? Friendly, too.

C'mon, baby, c'mon here—good boy! See, he really likes that. And they multiply so fast! Why, we'd have an infestation of minutes here in no time, if the hours didn't gobble 'em up 'most as fast as they breed.

That's the way it is here, you see, one big food chain. That's what makes being timekeeper not such a hard job. You just help 'em all keep passing along, that's all. Make sure the hours get their fill of minutes. The days, they fatten on hours. Fork a few days into the week's pen. Let the months prey on the weeks, till the year just sucks them up.

You see how it works. They all have their place, and they're all pretty nice, too. In their ways. Even the nanoseconds. You can't see them, of course, but you can hear their buzzing—if you listen real careful . . . Ayeh.

Out yonder there, we have a beautiful striped era. But he mostly just sleeps in the yard, next to the eon. Sometimes even I have trouble telling the difference 'tween those two.

Ah, look! Here comes my favorite! Upsa-daisy—that's a good girl! She's a fortnight. Furry little critter, friendliest of the whole bunch. She sleeps with me nights. Keeps me company days. We're pretty much inseparable, me and my fortnight.

I know. You're wondering, aren't you—how can I keep this one for my companion, when the rest of them are relentlessly gobbling each other up out there? Well, little Mobius here would be fattening up a month herself, 'cept I saved her for my next vacation.

Fade to black

"And the centuries! Why, the centuries, they just swallow you whole if you give 'em a chance —or even if you don't. Good thing there's only a few of them."

VERMONT LIFER

In 1986, writers Joe Citro, Roderick Bates, and Carl Yalicki; cultural entrepreneur Bill Schubart; and lawyer Stephen Blodgett assembled a parody of the state's semi-sacred self-promotional magazine, *Vermont Life*. With articles like "The Therapist Next Door" and "Village Idiots: Passing of an Era" and with a staff directory like that of the radio show *Car Talk,* they satirized the state on every page. Here's an abridged version of what they did with fishing.

HOW TO FISH LIKE A VERMONTER

A Treasury of Advice to the Fishing Flatlander

by J.Z. Siddy

In 1976, I moved from East Agent Orange, New Jersey, to Vermont. I had fish swimming in my imagination—images of misty lakes at sunrise and ice-cold mountain streams. I wanted to learn as quickly as possible all the tricks of angling in the Green Mountains. I wanted to fish like a true Vermonter.

What I learned, however, is that a Vermonter would sooner give up his guns, or the testicle of your choice, than part with any tips on the art of piscine pursuit.

Abandoned, I began to study not the habits of Vermont fish, but the habits of Vermont fishermen. Through careful observation I have learned a lot.

Following my instructions can save you time and humiliation. But more important, you'll soon be fishing like a true Vermonter.

> "What I learned, however, is that a Vermonter would sooner give up his guns, or the testicle of your choice, than part with any tips on the art of piscine pursuit."

ATTITUDE AND PHILOSOPHY

Developing a proper attitude is essential. One must learn to think like a Vermonter.

First, the purpose of fishing is to catch fish. Period. Forget sport, recreation, or relaxation—you're out there to bring home the bacon (or perch, pike, or whatever). Formalities like minimum length, daily limits, method of angling, and private property do not concern real Vermonters— they're merely ideas created by the Department of Fish and Game to keep Flatlanders from emptying our lakes and streams.

"NO TRESPASSING" signs, as everyone knows, are nailed up by only two types of people: real Vermonters, who don't want to look at a bunch of New Yorkers bumbling through the woods, and relocated Flatlanders who try to keep everyone away by purchasing all the land and "KEEP OUT" signs their money can buy.

Ignore the signs! Stomp right through those streams, park your truck wherever you desire. Greet anyone who challenges you with a simple "Hoi!" then turn and go about your business. Most Vermonters will recognize that you're "wunna 'nem boiz" (one of the boys) and leave you alone. Also, don't let the presence of a brandished firearm dampen your spirits. True Vermonters are oblivious to guns and do not let them influence their behavior. A good way to deal with someone with a shotgun is to shout, "Hey, 'zat a Mossberg bolt-action 20 gauge? Pretty noice. Got one m'self, in a 12!"

After lead sinkers were banned...

Loons took up smoking.

EQUIPMENT

Vermont sporting goods stores are full of rods, reels, lures, hooks, and lines of various types and descriptions. In reality, they are stocked primarily for Flatlanders. Flatlander companies, like Orvis, would have you believe that a fish can tell if you've got a $650 fly rod. The well-equipped Vermont fisherman wouldn't be caught dead with 80 percent of that crap. Keep this in mind: you must choose carefully, to outfit yourself in the Vermont tradition.

Rods: If you refer to a "fishing rod," it's already too late. To Vermonters, it's a "fish pole." Fish poles come in many sizes, but you want one at least six and a half to seven feet long, and sturdy enough not to break under extreme abuse. Don't concern yourself with matching pole and reel—the "designer" approach is for Flatlanders. Regardless of what type of reel you own, buy a spinning rod. Most Vermonters prefer salt water poles, though they don't realize it. In fact, most Vermonters don't realize there is salt water!

Reels: The only type to use is an inexpensive closed-face, push-button, spin-cast reel. Don't worry about drag settings, as long as you're able to snap heavy objects up out of the water. We highly recommend the Zebco 202. It's cheap, comes with heavy line, and can be easily stashed away in a drawer where it tangles or breaks. Get caught with a Ryobi or Shinomo Telflow Sensi-Strike spinning reel with its computerized memory drag, and you'll be forced south of Brattleboro so fast your head will spin.

Line: The minimally acceptable strength is eighteen pounds, although most Vermont fishermen prefer twenty-five. It has to be strong enough to rip out snagged tree limbs, tie down boats, or repair Chevys. Monofilament is okay, but many older Vermonters prefer "green cloth line, so's a man can see it."

There's only one bait to use in Vermont— night crawlers.

Lures: Forget 'em. There's only one bait to use in Vermont—night crawlers. These should not be purchased at a bait shop, but hand-picked or bought from someone with a misspelled advertisement in his dooryard. If you don't know what night crawlers are, pull up at the first run-down shack with such a sign, present the man with the advertised price—usually four cents—and ask him for one. Chances are, you'll also be able to observe a real Vermonter when he's pissed off.

If you must use lures, they should be well-weighted and with at least two treble hooks, perfect for snagging fish—the only thing a Vermonter would do with them.

Specialized Equipment: Any of the following will classify you as a real Vermonter:

- The use of canned corn for bait.

- Using Band-Aid boxes to store fishing tackle.

- The possession of a tin coffee can (can be used for crawlers, or to piss into while boating in a crowded lake).

- The possession of a cheap, beat-up hand gun.

Technique: Most Vermonters view the traditional fishing techniques from publications like *Field and Stream* as sheer horseshit. Such material is aimed at Flatlanders—who else would pay two dollars for a magazine?

Vermonters know that the best places to fish are easily driven to—they like to fish with the car nearby. Thus, the cooler of beer is handy. Another favorite spot of Vermonters is under a bridge. "Fish gotta swim under it. Ya never seen one pass over it, did ya?"

CONCLUSIONS

Forget the magazines, the books, and especially the fancy equipment outlets like L.L.Bean and Orvis—what they supply will only single you out as a foolish Flatlander. Though you may catch fish, you'll be scorned by those who really "Know."

To fish successfully in Vermont, you must rethink your entire approach. Keep it simple, just like a Vermonter.

You can't go wrong. Good luck.

IT'S ALL ABOUT LIVING[35]

from *How to Survive the Recession*

by Bob Stannard

VINCENT VAN GOGH   ROBERT STANNARD

Life is about living, unless you're really rich.

In the first chapter we discussed how it seems as though poor people focus on living more than rich people. Poor people, and I generalize here, don't pay much attention to the idea of dying. All right, they know they are going to kick off at some point, and it may nag at them in the back of their brain somewhere, but it's not like it's the biggest deal in their average day. They are preoccupied with avoiding pesky things like starvation, creditors, and things breaking that they might not know right-off how to fix and then having to go to a friend or neighbor and, heaven forbid, ask for help or advice. (For those of you who are not Vermonters, the only thing worse than dying is asking someone for help. We just don't do that here.)

Rich folk have got that, and just about everything else, covered. So, not having to be plagued with the regular day-to-day catastrophes of living, they have the luxury of simply worrying about dying. In addition, should they fly off the road in a snowstorm, they would think nothing of asking someone to help pull them out. A Vermonter would prefer to freeze to death in a position that indicated he was attempting to push the car out by himself. That would at least make the family proud.

Better be careful of what you eat, drink, wear, what stock you buy, locking your house, where you walk, and who you meet, because making a mistake can kill you. Then what? Then you're dead. Once you're dead, as they say, you can't take it with you, which implies that not only are you dead, but now you are broke, too. Perhaps the only thing more terrifying than dying for a rich person would be to face the reality of being broke for all eternity. Being dead and broke is too hard for rich people to even get their heads around. As of right now, thanks to this nasty recession, many people in this category are now broke and still alive. That ain't good. For the idle rich, death becomes the driving factor of day-to-day living.

That's why you see poor folks wandering right across the road without a care in the world. For that matter, poor people will take all kinds of risks, like going into strange bars, eating junk food, driving willy-nilly down the road in a snowstorm, sleeping on the sidewalk, or, in inclement weather, under a culvert. They'll drink beer while eating Cheez Whiz™ and riding snowmobiles.

The non-rich guy is busy praying that the motor mounts he replaced himself a week ago will remain in place as he's cruising down the highway at 80 miles per hour, so he doesn't have to face the prospect of the motor flying through the windshield. His concern would not be impending death by 500-pound motor, but that his friends and relatives would remember him as the dork who neglected to fully tighten the mounts.

Most poor people could care less if they check out. What the hell, where we're going can't possibly be worse than being here, can it? Islamic terrorists imagine being flocked around by seventy virgins. Poor Vermonters envision a heaven with a perpetually full woodbin and a roof that doesn't leak.

Watch out for that (fill in the blank), because it might kill us and then what? No more trips to Paris, no caviar, no wicked nice cars. You see, death for the rich brings all the good things to an end. Death for poor folks brings all the bad things to an end. They both reach the same end, but they are not likely to see it that way.

Makes you wonder if maybe being rich isn't all it's cracked up to be. To quote author David H. Sterry: "One of the unexpected benefits of the worst economic depression in a century is that, for the first time in history, poor people are happier than rich people. Experts claim this is because the lifestyle of poor people has barely changed with the downturn. They were below the poverty line before, and they're below the poverty level now." Bingo!

There you have it. Being rich, in the end, leaves you with nothing more than great anxiety about being poor.

Being poor, in the end, leaves you exhilarated at the prospect of going to a better place, a place where you know for certain the motor mounts are properly tightened down. Now, I know what you'll say— "Jeez, Bob, you're really full of beans." But guess what? There are boatloads more poor people in the world than there are rich people. Just do the math and bet on the horse most favored to win. Throw your money in your favorite swimming hole (or just send it to me). Shed the horrible burden and get with being poor and learn how to really live.

You see, it's not dying that's the problem; it's fear that's the problem.

THE MUD COMETH[36]
by Willem Lange

Starting in mid-February, the morning sun finally rises high enough in the sky to clear the rooftops on the south side of State Street in Montpelier and flood the front windows of the coffee shop on the north side. The clearest days are also the coldest, so we trot out the old New England aphorism, "February sun is hard won," and turn our faces toward it with our eyes closed.

But, by March we know that, just beneath our feet, that sun is creating a calamity—one we have to endure, all the while hoping it won't be too bad this year.

During the winter, the ground slowly freezes—though not as deeply as it used to—especially under the plowed roads, where there's no insulating blanket of snow. When the irresistible sun melts the frozen surface, the ice turns to water and the water looks for a drain, as water will. But the

ground beneath is still frozen, and will be for a while; the water's got nowhere to go, and the mixture turns to something like Dinty Moore® stew. Then somebody drives through it, and there goes your road.

It's impossible to describe mud season to anyone who's never experienced it—the uncertainty about whether you'll make it across to dry ground, the inability to steer, the sound of your muffler dragging across gravel and stones. Sometimes the mud freezes at night. That helps, unless, as the Maine humorist Tim Sample says, "You get cross-threaded in a couple of ruts."

I used to visit an old farmer in Etna, New Hampshire. He kept a pair of big horses for plowing, haying, logging, sugaring—and pulling cars out of mud holes. Just after the war, a doctor in Hanover bought a war surplus jeep, and used it for mud-season house calls. But he got stuck, anyway, and showed up at Elmer's door.

"I thought them things could go anywhere," Elmer said.

"Yep, they can," said the doc. "But they've gotta have at least one foot on solid ground."

Some of the old-time photographs of mud season and Model Ts stuck hub-deep are almost unbelievable. Nowadays, people carry cell phones, cameras, and GoPros, so we can experience their anxiety electronically: "Are we going to make it? If we don't, we're going to have to climb out into a foot of cold beef stew in our street shoes to go for help."

This is Willem Lange in Montpelier, and I gotta get back to work—assuming I can.

TURKEY DRIVES TO BOSTON[37]
by Peter Gilbert

Before railroads, the only way to get turkeys from Vermont to market in Boston was to walk them there. And that, throughout much of the nineteenth century, is exactly what Vermonters did, including Vermonters from the northernmost parts of the state. Townspeople put their birds of a feather together and, accompanied by wagons with camp supplies and tons of feed grain, they escorted as many as seven thousand birds at a time, all the way to Boston. Drives of three to four thousand birds were common in the 1820s and '30s. Historian Charles Morrow Wilson says that about one thousand birds was the minimum necessary to make the

NO HARM, NO FOWL

BOSTON 178 miles

BIG BIRDS, LITTLE BRAINS

150- to 350-mile trek worthwhile. It was a long haul. The flocks could make only ten to twelve miles a day, and at least one drover was required for each one hundred birds.

Boys scattered shelled corn feed in front of the birds, so they would walk forward, while others herded from behind. Flocks might spread out for more than a mile, ranging in width from a few feet to fifty yards. To protect the birds' feet on such a long hike over rough terrain and November's frozen ground, Vermonters sometimes coated the birds' feet with warm tar. They lost about ten percent of the turkeys to forded rivers, foxes, hungry farm families they met en route, and other perils of the journey.

Two key facts to keep in mind are: big birds, little brains. Wherever they were when the sun set, that's where they perched for the night. Their collective weight shattered trees. Occasionally, so many birds perched on a farmer's shed or barn that the building collapsed. They sometimes mistook the shade of a covered bridge for dusk and simply stopped. And so, the drovers would have to go in, pick them up, carry them through the bridge and into the sun, where they'd perk up again and head on their way.

The advent of railroads, and then, in the 1850s and '60s, refrigerated box cars, were the beginning of the end for the great turkey drives, but some lasted into the twentieth century. The notion, in the twenty-first century, of driving thousands of turkeys, or even two birds on a leash, from Island Pond south all the way to Boston is charming in its absurdity.

THE WINOOSKI[38]

by Adam Hall

Vermont Department of Health Cautions Residents Against Making Snow Angels After Reports of Ticks Wearing Tiny Coats and Hats

MONTPELIER—Children across the state are being warned by the Vermont Department of Health against lying down in the snow, thanks to new reports that ticks may be lurking just beneath the surface. While generally dormant in winter, ticks may be drawn to the comparative warmth of snow angels, and some people have reported seeing the ticks in winter gear.

A surge of Lyme disease has given a scare to any parents who still let their children outside from time to time, but many had believed that the winter was still a time of safety from the insects. Ticks can survive in harsh temperatures, but are dormant in temperatures under 35 degrees Fahrenheit (275 Kelvin).

"We urge caution and tick checks at all times, regardless of the season," said a statement released Friday morning. "Ticks are drawn to warmth, so activities like snow angels could lead to an increase in the chances for infection. And we are unsure how many ticks have been outfitted in winter gear, or who is supplying them with these items, but it may be that the ticks will be active in increasingly lower temperatures. As always, it is better to just never leave your house at any time."

While the increase in tick numbers and Lyme disease cases can be directly attributed to climate change, there is no information at this time regarding where the ticks are purchasing boots, hats, coats, and mittens.

VERMONT PEOPLE'S POET DAVID BUDBILL

The people's poet of Vermont, David Budbill, died before Adam Hall wrote his clever downer about ticks. But beloved Budbill would surely have responded with this uplifting poem:

Bugs in a Bowl

Han Shan, that great and crazy, wonder-filled
Chinese poet of a thousand years ago, said:
We're just like bugs in a bowl. All day going
around never leaving their bowl.
I say, That's right! Every day climbing up
the steep sides, sliding back.
Over and over again. Around and around.
Up and back down.
Sit in the bottom of the bowl, head in
your
hands, cry, moan, feel sorry for yourself.
Or. Look around. See your fellow bugs.
Walk around.
Say, Hey, how you doin'?
Say, Nice Bowl![39]

"Say, Hey, how
you doin'?

Say, Nice Bowl!"

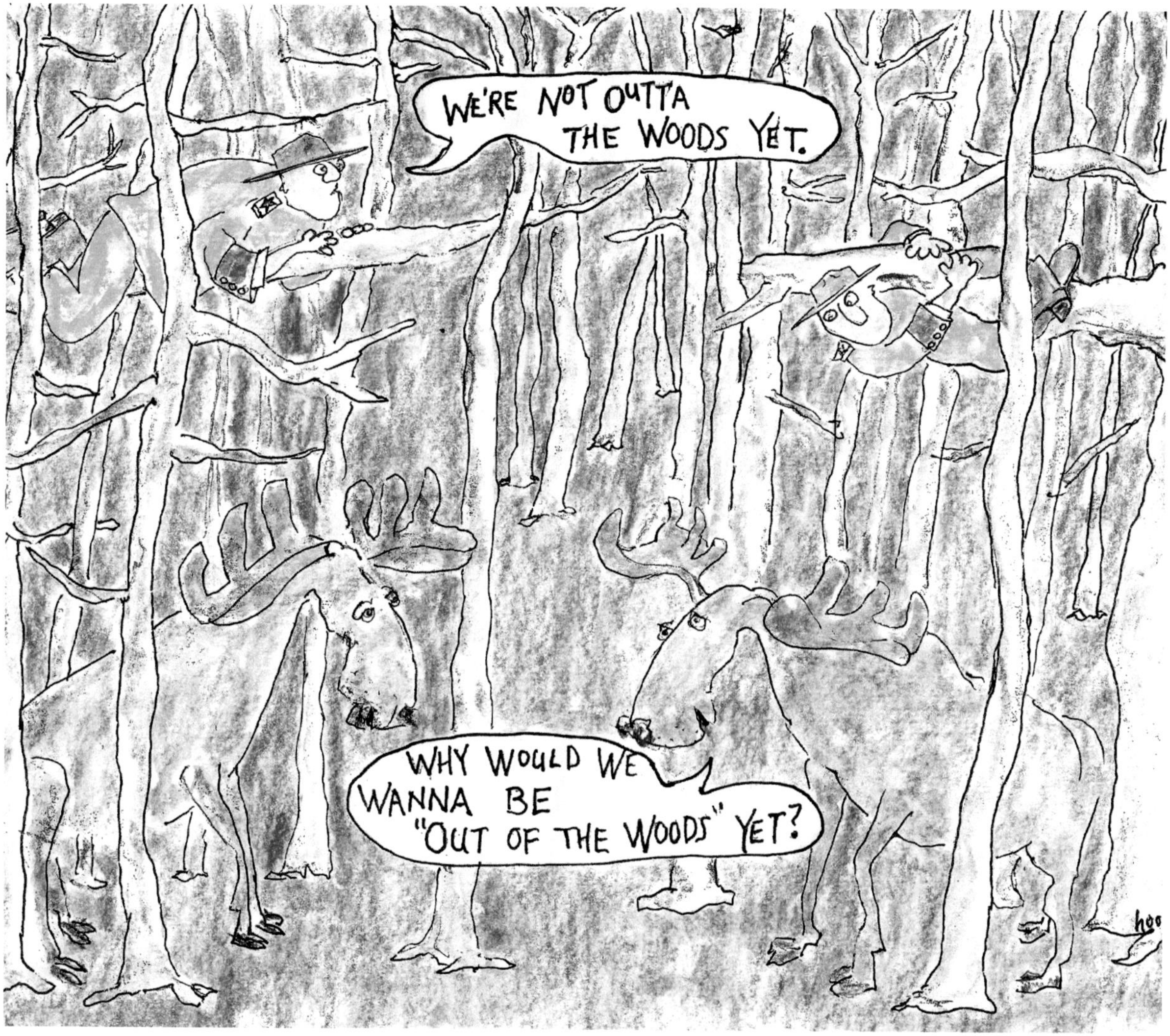
WE'RE NOT OUTTA THE WOODS YET.
WHY WOULD WE WANNA BE "OUT OF THE WOODS" YET?

CHAPTER 7

Alternative Universes

What ties the four acts in the previous chapter together?
They were and are groups and individuals who took to the stage to develop well-rounded personalities, which often cohered in one person playing different roles, or several people playing different roles. They kept reinventing themselves through their acting, music, skits, and the public events around them.

Danny Gore (aka Norm Lewis) created whole worlds out of whole cloth. His town of Avery's Gore, is a sort of Thornton Wilder *Our Town,* but with humor.

Ground Hog Opry spoofed the real Grand Ole Opry in Nashville.

Rusty DeWees took one character he'd played in a theater and turned it into a largely one-man show, to tour the state and New England.

And, in Hardwick, four friends formed a wildly popular variety show, Vermont Vaudeville, with a cast of locals and world-tour trippers.

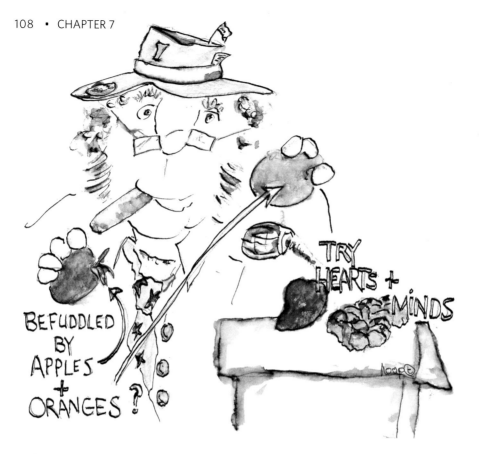

> **"Do a day's work. Tell the truth. Either one can make you sweat."**
>
> – Danny Gore

NORMAN LEWIS/DANNY GORE

Was he Norman Lewis or was he Danny Gore? "He was both," said journalist Rod Clarke about the dual personality of the Northeast Kingdom (NEK) sage.[40]

Norm Lewis was born on a ten-cow farm in Lunenburg, in Essex County. After hard work on the road crew and US Army service in Germany, he attended Lyndon Teachers College. He then worked his way up the education ladder from teacher to principal to superintendent in the Essex-Orleans supervisory district. In the summers of those years, he'd take his family to the White Mountains, where he ran and eventually managed the Mount Washington Cog Railway.

In the mid-1960s, while working as an unassuming school principal, Lewis split his own personality to create the character of Danny Gore, and the alternative universe of Avery's Gore. With Danny as the lead citizen, Lewis used the population-free Gore as his personal Petri dish to culture a virus of NEK humor and his own perennial candidacy for governor.

Lewis launched his character, Representative Lewis of Lewis, at a Chester, Vermont, PTA show, with a wild tie, and a long trench coat to hold his papers. "Representative" Danny Gore's vest came later, after he bought one to emcee at a Cog Railway party at Mount Washington. Later, he added a floppy fedora, campaign buttons of all sizes for all causes, an un-smoked cigar, and glasses perched on his nose in perpetual surprise or offense. Gore/Lewis gave over fifteen hundred performances and campaign appearances during the next thirty-plus years, as he mounted his quixotic biennial gubernatorial race. His "campaigns" allowed him to comment on the issues and people of the day, from the fictional residents of "the Gore," to genuine public figures, like the governor of the moment.

Some of the residents of the Gore included Grammy Zelda, the tireless Equal Rights Amendment proponent; Chip Hart, the Gore's token liberal; and Mark Bowker, who "walks" (not runs) the general store, since he doesn't move too fast. And then there's Cousin Castor, the poet laureate of the Gore, who "came into this world with very few adjustments. Some say God forgot to put a bubble in his level."

Lewis would talk impromptu, but always carried a stack of newspapers in an old canvas feed bag, and these would give him material when his memory flagged. His slogans varied from term to term, but the following were hardy perennials: "Do a Day's Work! Tell the truth! Either one can make you sweat."

For the first twenty years of his gubernatorial candidacies, he won 10-20-30 votes for "Danny Gore" but, in the mid-1980s, his votes disappeared into a category of results titled, "Scattered."

Danny's campaign promises were simple:

Positions not Polls

Issues not Image

Wisdom not Words

Common Sense not Consultants

Message not Media

Simple Language not Lawyers

Commitment not Committee

Decisions not Delegation

Policy not Politics

Facts not Fertilizer

"New Hampshire's motto is 'Live Free or Die,' Vermont's motto should be 'Work or Die.'"

Danny says, while New Hampshire's motto is "Live Free or Die," Vermont's motto should be "Work or Die."

No one escaped Danny's barb-less hooks:

TOPICAL TOPICS FROM WOODCHUCK'S POINT OF VIEW

To teachers: "We're sick of that 'would chuck could chuck wood' crap. How would you feel if we laid on you: 'How kind would mankind's kind be kind to his kind if mankind could be kind'?"

To radicals: "Why do skunks get all the attention just because they have no gray area, when everything is black or white?"

To vegetarians: "Don't laugh at woodchucks—my eating habits are not a fad."

To the Pentagon: "We prefer love with *no* light at the end of the tunnel."

To politicians: "At least when they had spittoons in the Vermont House, members displayed some coordination between brain and mouth."

To voters, on the school budget: "If you spawn 'em, you support 'em, or we'll spay ya!"

✦

At noon on November 8, 1994, after fifteen fruitless campaigns for governor, Danny Gore stood on the State House steps and *declared himself* governor. Seven minutes later, minutes he borrowed from the legally elected governor, Howard Dean, without the governor even knowing it, he abdicated the governor's seat and permitted Dean to serve out the remainder of his term.

Similar to Francis Colburn's fictional graduation speech, Danny Gore's *real* address to the graduates at Johnson State College in 1980 mixed wisdom and whimsy in a hearty stew of advice. His parting words were:

☛ **Don't be too busy to work.** We got some fellows up in the Gore, you go by their place and the only thing's working is hard cider. I say you ain't got a right to work; you have to work.

☛ **Set your goals.** Where are you goin'? Don't know where you're comin' from? Alvin, up in the Gore, he used to get potted so he could speak with geraniums.

We got Cousin Castor up there. You've heard of the rainbow connection, the French Connection? Well Castor is our loose connection. He wanted to lasso airplanes. His goal in life was to get one of those airplanes. He'd hear it, he go out there, and he'd throw the lasso at the airplane 'til it was out of sight. After he came back in the house, they'd ask him, "How come you missed your goal?" And he said, "The sun was in my eyes."

Now there's an excuse for not reaching your goal . . . but you gotta have faith. Town folks had faith in Castor there—they chipped together and got him a parachute . . . just in case he met his goal.

There is no such thing as a risk-free society. You never heard of a blacksmith being successful shoeing dead horses. Be a leader, or a follower. Both of 'em are just as important.

Be a class that has class. Be proud of graduating from Johnson. You are somebody from somewhere. The obligation you have is only to make the planet a better place. I'm pleased you asked me to speak, and I'm sure by now some of you are asking yourself, "Well, did Danny do as well as we expected?"

"Well, no he didn't. But then, again, we didn't expect he would."

Thank you.[41]

> "And then there was Cousin Castor who came into this world with very few adjustments. Some say God forgot to put a bubble in his level."

GROUND HOG OPRY[42]

Since the mid-1990s, one of the funniest places to be during mud season in Vermont has been a school gym or auditorium, when Ground Hog Opry brought its (some-annual) revue to town.

The radio-style musical variety show has been part of the back-side of Vermont entertainment landscape since Ground Hog Day, 1991. This Vermont parody of Nashville's Grand Ole Opry was the brainchild of Waterbury farmer/actor/musician George Woodard, who introduces himself as Roland Uphill: "Woodchuck, Vermont, is a town that's a little rough, not all that pretty a place—but just kind of a workin' place where regular people live."

By 1995, Woodard teamed up with Al Boright, a lawyer for the legislature (aka Neal Down), and took Ground Hog Opry on its initial tour, titled "The 17th Annual" tour, to be followed two years later by "The 19th Annual."

Ground Hog Opry (GHO) became part 1940s radio-variety show, part "Bob and Ray," part *Saturday Night Live,* part *Prairie Home Companion,* part Capitol Steps, and part *Hee Haw,* with lots of music thrown in, both country standards and original satire. It broad cast from station WSMM ("Well Shut My Mouth!"— a cherished line which knowing audiences shout back to the performers).

The show was centered around the fictitious run-down village of Woodchuck, Vermont, plus a few surrounding towns, such as Peckerville, Most Peculiar, and More-or-Lessville. Al Boright does fake news casts, and conjures up a host of outrageous advertisements and special skits, like Barnyard Olympics—including a "manure pit half-pipe."

Boright grew up in Morrisville, where his father was superintendent of schools. Like Woodard, he was active in school musicals. Boright went on to Harvard, to Vietnam as an officer, and then to law school. He described his Vietnam experience, where he was badly wounded, in a one-man show called "Woodchuck Warrior." A news junkie, who saw humor everywhere, Boright had to choose his targets carefully while writing laws for politicians of all stripes and egos. Still, his zingers recalled the acid tongue of another Harvard graduate, Tom Lehrer.

The pair built up a company which included a son and nephew of Woodard's, one John Drury, a virtuoso multi-instrumental traditional musician; Carrie Cook, an artist, on upright bass; Nancy MacDowell on vocals; Jim Pitman on dobro; and actress Ramona Godfrey; and even, for a while, Vermont Supreme Court Justice Marilyn Skoglund.

So far, GHO toured during twelve different calendar years, most recently in 2017.

Entertainer, folk singing guitarist, and dairy farmer, George Woodard of Waterbury, has a stand-up riff that goes something like this:

> Farmer Keith Sprague and fourteen-year-old daughter Annabelle are in the barn for morning milking. It's a cold March day, 6:30 AM. Annabelle is feeding calves when she discovers old Bessie, a beloved

"Well Shut My Mouth radio (WSMM) is brought to you by Eeeeeewwww Flatlander-Repellant Breath Mints in four repulsive flavors. Chomp on a Yesterday's Fish today."

twelve-year-old Holstein who'd been ailing, has died during the night.

    Distressed, Annabelle bawls out to her dad: "Pawh, Bessie's dead!"

    Unstated, but obvious to any Vermont farm daughter—it's early March. The ground is frozen solid. They can't bury Bessie.

    Continued distress: "Pawh, what should we do?"

Farmer Sprague reflects, calls back from the stanchion where he's milking, "Get the Massey. Hitch 'er up. Drag ole Bess out by the mailbox and put a 'FREE' sign on her."

A SELECTION OF GHO'S ADVERTISING WIT

After Disaster Builders

This is Buster Bridges for After Disaster Builders. If you become a victim of a flood, tornado, earthquake, wildfire, or other natural disaster that is bad enough to make the select board suspend the building ordinances so as to expedite rebuilding of the community, you are a fool if you aren't thinking of After Disaster Builders.

If the standards get low, let us know. We're ready to go, give us the dough, and ask no mo'. Our competitors can't match our low prices or our high speed out of town. That's After Disaster Builders. You won't find us in no phone book, we'll contact you. After the disaster.

All Test Taking Services

We'd like to welcome our new sponsor, All Test Taking Services. If you have an important test you're facing, and you're nervous, and you dread the dickens out of it, then just call All Test. Facing college boards? A driving test? A urine test? A sobriety test? A blood test? An eye test? An acid test? High test? A test of wills? A test of your emergency network? Just call our experienced team of experts, and we'll be right there.

Yes folks, we're talking All tests. Like the name says.

You fake 'em. We take 'em.

Bring us in and you win.

That's All Test Taking Services.

Woodchuck Yankee Exempt Estates

This part of the show is brought to you by Woodchuck Yankee Exempt Estates, the new multipurpose commercial operation inside the Woodchuck Yankee Fence. Since the federal court held that state law was entirely preempted at Woodchuck Yankee, we've got:

"If the standards get low, let us know. We're ready to go, give us the dough, and ask no mo'."

Housing: The company offers affordable, preheated housing you could die for, at costs that are so reasonable because no expensive state laws need be complied with. No expensive fire codes or drinking water standards, and none of those picky electricity regulations. Let the juices flow, mofo. It's all good . . . er, good profit.

Racing: Drive your own racecar, anywhere inside the fence.

Drinking: Drivers' license suspensions and liquor license requirements don't apply here.

Old Tire Pyre and Junk Car Disposal: Residents enjoy free tire disposal at our new firepit, and you can drop off that junk car you was thinking of pushin' over the edge of the Peckerwood quicksand pit.

Gambling: We been gambling here for decades, now we're just gonna expand to include conventional games of chance.

Rock Concert Venue: No noise standards apply, so the doors are open for business.

Professional Services: We have super deals in any state-licensed professional services. Again, save with our accountants, engineers, architects, physical and mental health professionals . . .

Eeeeeewwww. Flatlander-Repellant Breath Mints

Did you ever want to be left alone?

Are you a cashier at a small store, and you have never found the right way to get revenge on your boss?

Did you ever want to get even with your dental hygienist for being so rough when cleaning your teeth?

Are you claustrophobic, but you'd like to go to the championship games anyway, even though it's bound to be wall-to-wall people?

Fly-by-Night Industries proudly introduces: Eeeeeewwww. Flatlander-Repellant Breath Mints.

Eeeeeewwww comes in four flavors:

> Unflossed Green Jaw
> Yesterday's Fish
> Cowpie with Onion
> Stale Cigarette Butted in Bud

And the smell only lasts ten minutes per breath mint. That's Eeeeeewwww. Flatlander-Repellant Breath Mints.

RUSTY DEWEES, "THE LOGGER"[43]

Rusty DeWees's alternative universe is both artistic and commercial. Born in Philadelphia, but raised in Stowe, Vermont, he's been a gas jockey, race car driver, basketball player and coach, musician, and concrete worker. He has been an author, actor, artist, auctioneer, agent, advertiser, and more.

Rusty found the stage as a young adult, when he discovered Vermont Repertory Theatre and its director, Robert Ringer. Later, he acted in several Lamoille County Players shows before moving to New York City, where he trained at the George Loris Actors Theatre School and the Lee Strasberg

One Belgian saison,
one Edward draft;
who ordered the Logger?

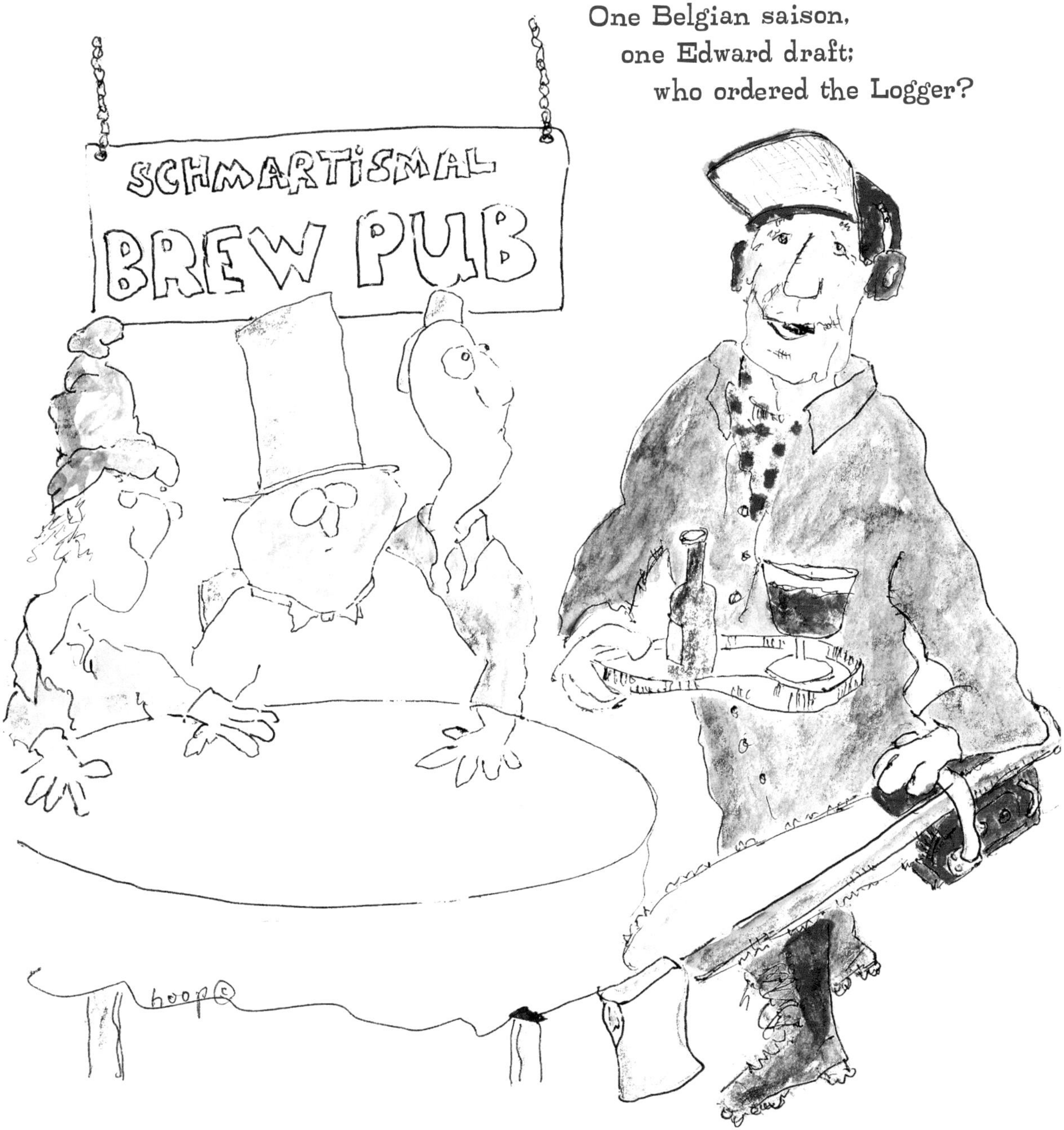
SCHMARTISMAL
BREW PUB
hoop©

Institute. This training led to work off-Broadway, as well as in television, film, and national commercials.

For a decade in New York, Rusty's day job was at the William Doyle Galleries. As the proprietor's right-hand man, he lapped up all he could. He said, "Bill Doyle taught me mostly everything I know about business: *'Call back! Bring the food! It's not yesterday; it's tomorrow!'*"

When he moved back to Vermont, Rusty continued his acting career and developed a one-man comedy show called *The Logger,* based roughly on the character he memorably played in David Budbill's play *The Chain Saw Dance.* The show opens with a pantomime of him starting up a recalcitrant chain saw with sound effects aplenty. He scratches, swears, frowns, scowls, and occasionally smiles. "Freakin'," "friggin'," and "frickin'" are frequent adjectival friends. Antoine, the logger, is a witty, scatological, French-Canadian lumberjack. "Obviously, I didn't learn The Logger from Chekhov or from Sam Shepard; I learned how to do The Logger from David Budbill, believe me," said DeWees.

To the acting, he added paid and pro bono radio ads for a variety of clients and causes. He produced three Logger DVDs, two CDs, five calendars, Logger apparel (duct tape wallets, caps, T-shirts, and hoodies) and two book-length collections of newspaper columns: *Scrawlins* and *Scrawlins, Too.* Rusty also conceived an augmented show called *The Logger and the Fiddler.* The "fiddler" was Vermont-born, fifth-generation fiddler Patrick Ross, who has performed at the Grand Ole Opry and shared stages with Willie Nelson, Johnny Cash, and Paul McCartney.

In the following piece, Rusty, the jokester, reveals some of his secrets.

> He scratches, swears, frowns, scowls, and occasionally smiles. "Freakin'," "friggin'," and "frickin'" are frequent adjectival friends.

JOKE TIPS from Rusty DeWees[44]

Laughing is curious. How/why does something you hear, read, think about, or see cause your body to conjure up a laugh? I certainly don't know, and that's fine, it's not my job to know.

My job is to make folks laugh. That's why, I think, I'm often approached by random people who want to tell me a joke. Every now and then, I'm thrilled someone comes out with a really good one. Most often the jokes folks tell fall a little flat. I'm not complaining. It's not their fault and I'm not saying they aren't necessarily good at telling jokes. It may be I'm not easily amused. At least not by jokes.

As a public service, the following are tips you can work on that might make your joke-telling more effective.

• Don't start your joke by saying, "Here's one you'll like."

• Don't approach the joke tellee all proud, as if you're about to whisper to them the cure for cancer.

• Know the joke you're telling cold. To say, "Oh wait, I forgot how it goes," is not acceptable. Remember, effective joke telling is serious business. "Failing to prepare is preparing to fail" applies here.

• Do not get too up in the physical space of the person you are telling the joke to.

• Regardless of the space you've left between you and that person, you should have good-smelling breath.

• Do not telegraph the punch line. In other words, tell the story and let the joke work on its own.

- Do not discount your abilities. "I heard this joke, it was funny. I'll tell it to you, but I'm not very good at telling jokes." Every time Pavarotti had a cold, he didn't hold up a sign that said, "I know a song, it's a good one, I'll sing it for you, but I have a cold." If you want to tell a joke, commit. Besides, making excuses puts the attention on you, not where it should be, which is solely on the joke.

- You don't need to smile the whole time while telling the joke; in fact, don't smile at all, unless you're playing a character in the joke and that character is a smiler.

- If you must tell a dirty joke, be sure your audience is game. I think dirty jokes are less funny, but it's all subjective.

- Vary the tempo of the lines in the joke. Don't rush it, and don't end each line saying, "ya got it"—"So there's this dry fern talking to a cat . . . ya got it?"—"Hey, kitty, can you get me some water?—ya got it?" Don't do that. *You got it?*

- Once you've reached the crucial moment just before the punch line of the joke, burp, break wind, cough, wheeze, barf, cry, do all those things if you must, but please, please don't laugh.

- It can work if you tailor the joke (change the words) to fit your telling abilities and overall sensibilities, but you should, as much as possible, tell the joke in the manner in which it was intended to be told.

- Most crucial is for you to remember that you're not funny, the joke is.

Rusty DeWees violates his own JOKE TIP #13. He preaches "most crucial is for you to remember that you're not funny, the joke is." The Logger is hilarious as he chainsaws pretension to bits.

See how many of the tips you can utilize while telling the following joke:

A guy got a new hearing aid and was all happy and proud
and bragging, and told his friend, "Hey, I got a new hearing aid."
The friend said, "What kind is it?"
The guy said, "It's 10:15."

That's a perfect joke to tell to hone your skills, because all you have to do is say the words.

Thanks, and as my dad used to tell me as we walked down his path to my car, "Make 'em laugh."

VERMONT VAUDEVILLE

Since 2008, the Hardwick Town House has been the home of a madcap, headlong, biannual variety show of juggling, mime, puppets, pratfalls, pogo stick jumping, storytelling, and even ballet. Performing before a lovingly-restored, hundred-year-old painted theater curtain displaying a romantic scene of the Alps, Vermont Vaudeville offers a compelling blend of the spontaneous, the sketchy, and the finely wrought, all for maximum effect. With its motto of "Laugh Locally," even an insane gorilla hardly seems out of place.

Vermont Vaudeville takes pleasure in the unexpected, with performances designed to disrupt the mundane, defy the logical, and relish in the absurd. The show is as tight as an atom and as loose as a pillow fight.

Justin Lander, one of the founders and emcee of the show, is a comedian, puppeteer, musician, and auctioneer. An alum of Bread and

Puppet Circus, he has toured with puppet shows nationally and internationally since 2002, and has been "Professor of Mr. Punch" since 2006. He teaches workshops for kids and adults in puppetry, junk music, and improv comedy. He also plays the musical bicycle pump.

Rose Friedman, Lander's partner and co-founder of Vermont Vaudeville, has been working in theater since she was a child. She studied at the Moscow Art Theater and The New School in New York City. Also an alum of Vermont's Bread and Puppet, she continues to work as a teaching artist for all ages. She sings and plays a wicked ukulele.

Brent McCoy, a third founder, has juggled and pogo-sticked around the world since 2005. He has appeared at numerous international busking, fringe, clown, and vaudeville festivals, as well as colleges, schools, and special events throughout the United States.

Maya McCoy, Brent's partner and fourth Vermont Vaudeville founder, has performed since she was in kindergarten. She also studied theater at The New School. She is a juggler, clown, and physical comedian with seemingly limitless facial expressions.

Also in the core troupe is musician Otto Muller, who got his start at age sixteen, playing jazz piano under an assumed name at casinos, bars, restaurants, and mafia Christmas parties in upstate New York. Muller is a composer of delicately uncomfortable avant-garde chamber music, and a faculty member at Vermont's Goddard College.

Greg Jukes is a narrator and percussionist whose work focuses on blending music, acting, and dance in hybrid arts performances. Greg has performed across the country with his hybrid arts ensemble, The Fourth

With its motto of "Laugh Locally," even an insane gorilla hardly seems out of place.

"I arise in the morning torn between a
desire to save the world and
a desire to savor the world. . ."
— E.B. White

Wall, and has been part of large-scale performances around Boston, as a member of Kadence Arts.

Vermont Vaudeville's "grassroots variety show" has grown at both ends of the talent scale, mixing local amateurs with globe-trotting professionals, and a lot in between.

Said Lander: "We have to keep setting the bar higher, because the audience expects things they haven't seen before. Our guest performers come from all over the world, and bring outrageous and delightful spectacle and skill. We curate the shows, so no two acts are alike. Each show is a balance: familiar characters and never-before-seen performers; timely local jokes and classic bits; original topical songs and jazz standards; stand-up comedy and death-defying stunts."

They all have day jobs, performing individually or in other groups, traveling around the country and the world following their own creative parabolas only to return "home" for another Vermont Vaudeville show.

To the members of Vermont Vaudeville, education is at least as important as entertainment. They offer workshops, school performances, and artists residency programs. During the quarantine, they did private performances—not on Broadway, but in your driveway.

Says Brent: "The emphasis is actually on fun. Yeah, we are dedicated to the preservation of live entertainment as an art form in the digital age, and I'm sure that has educational value, but we believe there is cultural value to doing this. There's inspiration potential when you bring three hundred students together who don't know each other, just to have fun with live entertainers."

"To build here this … slice of Vermont where the old and the new can exist happily."

Their dual mission is to build both a physical community and a human community, which will keep coming back. At every show, they pass the hat to help pay for further restorations to the building: re-painting, installing new lights and an electrical system, improving the dressing rooms, and plumbing, etc. This enlightened self-interest certainly helps Vermont Vaudeville, but also anyone who uses the Town House space. As Brent McCoy says, "The crown jewel of this whole project is that this historic building has found new life."

"We've developed a relationship with the audience," says Friedman. "It's not just one slice of the community that comes. Everybody feels welcome. I don't want to let that go anytime soon."

And, as Lander observed: "We've tried, since the beginning, to make this performance an open space for all Vermont, the New Vermont, the Old Vermont, the left, the right—that's the mission— to be wide open, to make this space live and be open, never to be exclusive, to build here this microcosm, this slice of Vermont where the old and the new can exist happily in parallel universes. What all of Vermont is, we want it to get in the door, where all of Vermont can be welcomed through the door."

Wilmer had to finally concede that he'd actually never had a dog that would hunt.

To Every Complicated Problem There is a Simple Solution

And, Quite Possibly, It's Wrong.

— H.L. Mencken

Meanwhile, over in New Hampshire

CHAPTER 8

Vermont vs. New Hampshire: A Tale of Cain and Abel

In 2000, at the request of a farmer friend who raised kale, Montpelier, Vermont entrepreneur Bo Muller-Moore designed and started printing his trademark green "Eat More Kale" T-shirts. Distinctively emblematic of Vermont's counterculture self-image, the T-shirts caught on. A decade later, the artist businessman applied for a trademark to protect his successful product. At which point, Chick-fil-A, the second largest fried chicken retailer in the US, sued Muller-Moore, claiming his slogan encroached on their "Eat Mor Chikin" tagline.

A true David vs. Goliath tilt ensued, with underdog kale winning hearts as tone-deaf corporate Chick-fil-A tried to bully Bo out of business. Even Vermont Governor Peter Shumlin backed Bo, as Eat More Kale became the shibboleth for Vermonters and hip tourists alike. Kale prevailed in 2014!

We got! We got!...

Correctly, in both my and Don's opinion, there's a delicious rivalry between Vermont and New Hampshire. Adjacent states, comparable in size, each considers its neighbor as a sort of upside-down version of itself. In attitude, culture, national significance, even wealth, each considers itself somewhat joyously superior to its mirror image.

Here, for example, might be a neighborly joust between Warren of Walpole (New Hampshire) and Brayton of Bellows Falls (Vermont):

Warren, shouting across the Connecticut: "Say, Brayton, you really ought to come over to New Hampshire sometime, see what we got that's superior."

Brayton: "Oh, w'all, what's that, Warren?"

Warren: "W'all, we got two Congress people. You only got one. We got four hundred Reps in our Legislature, you only got a hundred fifty. We got lotta money an no taxes, big ole mansions, and new-money McMansions. We got a real ocean; you only got a not-so-Great Lake. An' now, with the downcountry world bein' such-all pandemicked, we got high rollers rollin' in from Beacon Hill an Wall Street. W'all, we got, we got . . ."

Brayton, interrupting politely, "Pretty impressive, Warren, but we got somethin' in Vermont you don't have."

Warren, disbelieving, shouts back across the river: "Oh yeah, and what would that be, Brayton?"

Brayton, modestly smug, stage whispers, "We got ENOUGH."

Adjacent states, comparable in size, each considers its neighbor as a sort of upside-down version of itself.

Vermont Hustle

A hard hat from Manchester, New Hampshire, complains about doing some construction work in Manchester, Vermont. "There's no such thing as 'hustle' in Vermont. In New Hampshire (or New York, or New Jersey…), at 6:30 AM, at a diner, there's always twenty-five eggs on the griddle, because the cook knows the early birds want their egg sandwiches. In Vermont, there can be a line of fifteen people out the door, and the breakfast cook will put one organic, free-range, well-loved egg on the grill at a time."

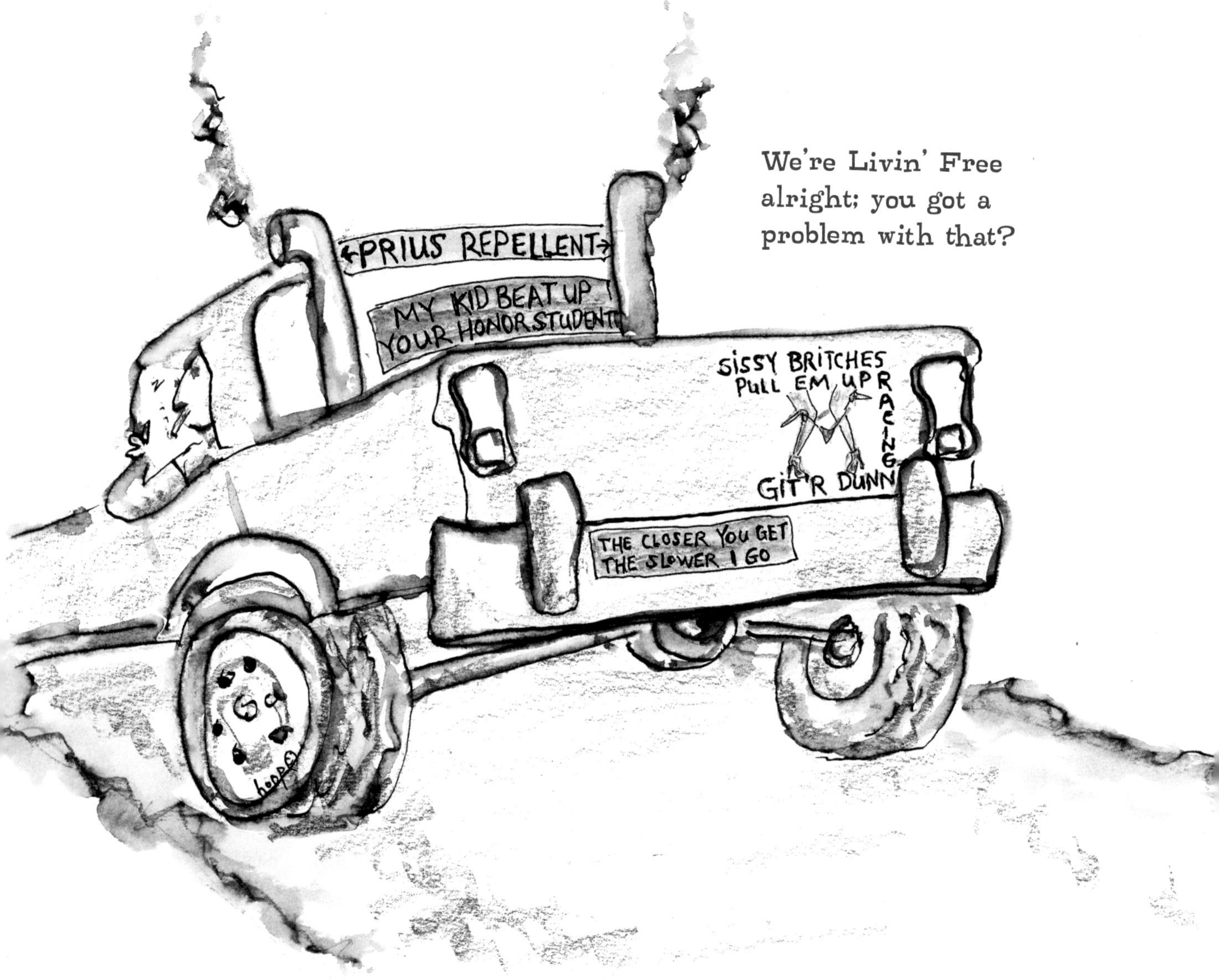
←PRIUS REPELLENT→
MY KID BEAT UP YOUR HONOR STUDENT
SISSY BRITCHES PULL EM UP
RACING
GIT'R DUNN
THE CLOSER YOU GET THE SLOWER I GO

We're Livin' Free alright; you got a problem with that?

John McCullough's Ode to New Hampshire

(Freewheeling thoughts while following a New Hampshire car down a straight and narrow road, being free-verse with liberty and license, too.)

Blessings on thee,
Little State.
Wearing your patriotism
On your license plate.
No hard-bitten Yank is supposed to believe

In wearing his heart
Upon his sleeve.
Then what sort of faith is this we keep—all sloganized
And just tin-deep?
LIVE FREE OR DIE, the tin plate states.

Die?
Free?
I?
Who, he?
Why?
Me???
Me, free?
Free, for instance, to expurgate—or otherwise, obliterate this
tin commandment,

Which this State feels free enough to legislate,
And put upon the license plate
Of every "free" man in the State

The State states "No," I'm not that free,
Such freedom is a state offense, with time in jail as consequence,
And freedom doesn't long prevail
In jail.

How free, then, must I try to be, or
Worse yet, be compelled to be,
If I don't try to not comply
Then must I
Die!

I cry thy help, oh gentle reader—pray take me to your *Union-Leader*.

Yet—come to think of it,
I am free.
As free, perhaps, as man ought be.
My patriotism I need not vaunt,
Unless I want.
You see, I'm living
In Vermont.

✦

INDEED, WE DO COMMIT RANDOM ACTS of KINDNESS + SENSELESS ACTS of BEAUTY

so what if THE HOKEY-POKEY IS WHAT IT'S ALL ABOUT

Transplant: Helen Highwater

Most years, the Connecticut River, which separates Vermont from New Hampshire, floods dramatically with the spring snowmelt from both the Green and White Mountains. Lifelong Vermonter Helen Highwater had lived most of forty years on a spit of land jutting into the river, near Newbury, Vermont.

About a decade ago, climate change began to seriously assert itself as early as Town Meeting Day—the first Tuesday in March. That year, the normally docile and contrite Connecticut became so wild, upset, and furious, it gouged and scoured its way violently south. Enormous hunks of riverbank streamed downstream, and Helen's little Vermont peninsula was no match for the raging river.

For nearly a week, Helen monitored her survival chances as the determined river rose, relentlessly shrinking her now-island homestead. Eventually, however, her Vermont grit prevailed. The rain stopped. The brilliant March sun came out. The water receded. And sure enough, lo and behold, Helen Highwater became the news story of the year. After living her entire life as a Vermonter, Helen on her little spit, found herself attached to the eastern shore of the Connecticut. The media descended.

"How does it feel to 'Live Free or Die,' Ms. Highwater, after living your whole life (so far!) as a Green Mountaineer?"

"W'all, I never could stand them frigid Vermont winters," conceded the sad transplant.

To which a New Hampshire bystander chirped, "Ayah, we've heard them wintahs are long and hard, but we understand Vermont makes up for 'em with low wages and high taxes."

> "Ayah, we've heard them wintahs are long and hard, but we understand Vermont makes up for 'em with low wages and high taxes."

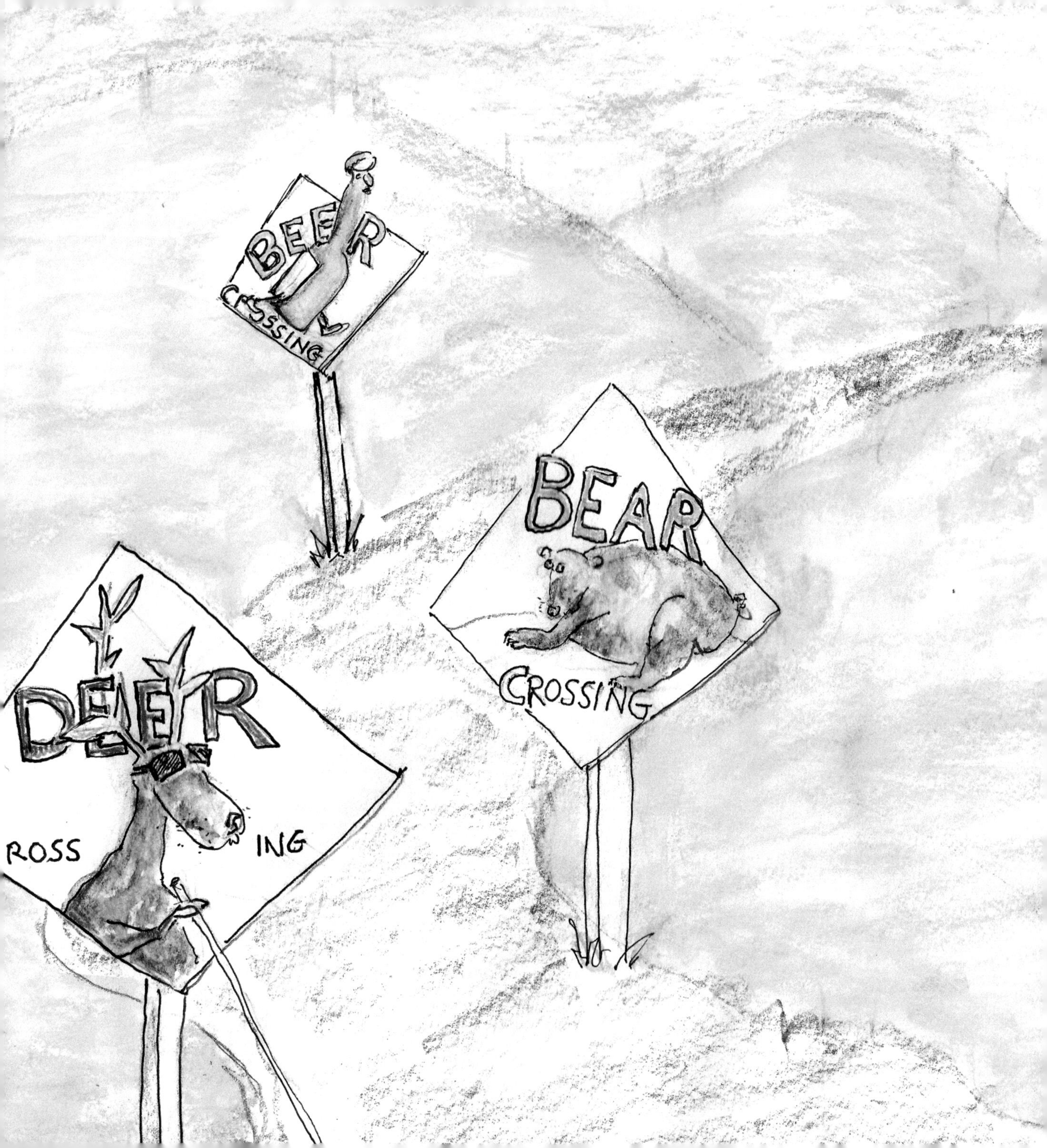
BEER
CROSSING
BEAR
CROSSING
DEER
ROSS ING

Vermonters know "summer" is a noun, not a verb

New Hampshire poet Donald Hall, poet laureate of both New Hampshire and the United States, once wrote:

"Heaven knows, Vermont is a beautiful state, with pockets of real country remaining, but it is the chic northern New England rural retreat, not New Hampshire.... To Vermont go summering professors of philosophy, Dada poets from New Jersey, and CEOs. The result is Woodstock, where orthopedic surgeons wear checked shirts from L.L.Bean, and play at being country folk, in the spirit of Marie Antoinette dressing up as a milkmaid."[45]

Most of all, Real Vermonters never, ever try to look like Real Vermonters.

Latte-drinking, sushi-eating,... left-wing freak show

In January 2004, Vermont Governor Howard Dean was surging to Democratic front-runner in that year's presidential race to unseat incumbent President George H. W. Bush. An Iowa television ad, paid for by the conservative tax cut organization Club for Growth, sought to hobble Dean by branding Vermont as irredeemably, unforgivably Liberal. The group's message was that Dean is an extremist.

Unidentified Female: "What do you think of Howard Dean's plans to raise taxes on families by $1,900 a year?"

Unidentified Male: "What do I think? Well, I think Howard Dean should take his tax-hiking, government-expanding, latte-drinking, sushi-eating, Volvo-driving, *New York Times*-reading ..."

Unidentified Female: "Body-piercing, Hollywood-loving, left-wing freak show back to Vermont, where it belongs."

"So, *take that!* Howard Dean and your Freedom and Unity Vermont!"

New Hampshire gourmet cachet? Not so much.

Interestingly, just four years earlier, in the 2000 presidential campaign between candidates George H. W. Bush and Vice President Al Gore, the Republican team tried to paint Vermont as "unapologetically antibusiness." National Public Radio's Linda Wertheimer asked Vermont Creamery president and co-founder, Allison Hooper, whether it was difficult to manufacture cheese under Vermont's reputedly strong environmental regulations. In effect, the query was, "Why, for heaven's sake, don't you move across the river to biz-friendly New Hampshire?" Hooper returned the zinger, closing the argument with, "New Hampshire Butter & Cheese Company just doesn't have the same cachet."

I ♥ VERMONT
by Alec Hastings

Be forewarned—this article is Vermont-centric. Also, it starts right off with sacrilege. Here it is: The most important part of being a Vermonter is not being born in Vermont. Now, don't get your hackles up and your overalls in a twist, all you sixth-generation Vermonters. Ponder this question from Francis Colburn before you light your kindling with this paper: "If your cat had kittens in the oven, would you call them biscuits?" I know. You're wondering who the heck Francis Colburn is, and what your cat was doing in the oven in the first place. Well, Francis was a University of Vermont art professor and a Vermont humorist, many years ago. As to the cat—this was back in the days of wood-burning cook stoves. Maybe Mother started a fire in the morning when the house was cold and let it go out, but she left the oven door open and Tabby found a nice, warm spot to have her babies. The point is this: being born in Vermont doesn't make you a Vermonter any more than being born in the oven makes you a biscuit. Being a Vermonter isn't just about where you were born; it's about what kind of person you are.

If you wonder where you stand on the Vermontometer, let's chuck your birth certificate and look at some other measures. Do you bleed maple syrup when you get cut? Would you gladly trade coq au vin or caviar for baked beans and pork? When you hear the word "farm," do you feel a tug on

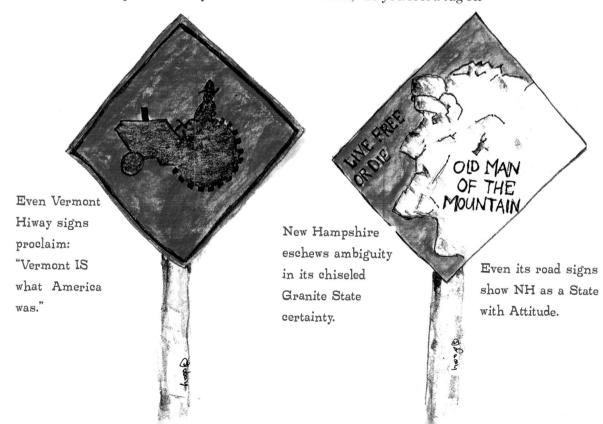

Even Vermont Hiway signs proclaim: "Vermont IS what America was."

New Hampshire eschews ambiguity in its chiseled Granite State certainty.

Even its road signs show NH as a State with Attitude.

your heartstrings? Do you like living in a state where "Gut Deer?" bumper stickers cross swords with those saying "Eat More Kale"? Do you remember the slogan "Spread Fred" with fondness? When you re-cross that Vermont state line after being "away," do you feel like you've just returned to God's country? If you answered yes to any of these questions, read on. You might be a Vermonter at heart, even if you were born in Quincy, Mass. If you don't aspire to this elite status . . . Lord love a duck! What's wrong with you? Here's the recipe for a true Vermonter.

You have heard that Vermonters are independent. I know this for a fact, because, as a high school English teacher in Bethel, Vermont (an outpost of real Vermonters), my students sometimes told me, "I'm a Vermonter and I do what I want-er!"

I also remember the story about my Vermont grandfather getting his fingers crushed between two steel rollers in a Ryegate paper mill, circa 1920. The doctor said he'd have to amputate Gramp's fingers. My grandfather said no, so the doctor scrubbed Gramp's said fingers with iodine and a vegetable brush. Gramp kept his fingers—albeit a little crooked—and was digitally able for the rest of his life. Yes, Vermonters are independent—some might even say stubborn or contrary.

Alongside the independent streak in Vermonters is a mother lode of ingenuity. Phrases like "cob together" and "jury rig" entered the Vermont lexicon because of the Vermonter's penchant for unorthodox repairs and "making do," as in, "Use it up, wear it out, make it do, or go without." Those were words to live by in the days of hillside farms. In the days before fuel-injected car engines were invented, I saw Vermont ingenuity firsthand

"Do you bleed maple syrup when you get cut? Would you gladly trade coq au vin or caviar for baked beans and pork?"

A VERMONT RIG

An' 'nother thing. They try to tell you "DAYS ARE GITTIN' LONGER IN JANUARY," that's a total crock.

when a friend's car wouldn't start. He was on his way to be best man at his brother's wedding, so this was a serious situation. Fortunately, my buddy Sid Hoyt had a knack for tinkering. Popping the hood, he noticed gas leaking around the bottom of the carburetor. He bought a jumbo pack of gum, crammed all the sticks in his mouth at once, and chewed like a dog with a steak. Then he plucked the giant wad from his mouth, and jammed it into the gap between the carburetor and the intake manifold, where a piece of gasket was missing. My friend turned the key, the engine roared to life, and off he drove in triumph.

Vermonters are a tolerant lot, too. No, not all of them, you naysayers! I'm talking about the *best* Vermonters, the role models. Their credo is "Live and let live." I will draw again on Vermonters' vocabulary for evidence. When I was growing up in the 1950s, I remember my elders using the word "rig." Rig can be a verb, as in "I will rig a tripod to hoist that engine." It can be a noun, as in "Mister Jimmy Johnson has a new sugaring rig." There is, however, a special Vermont use of the word, as in "Thaddeus is quite a *rig,* isn't he?" Rig in that context means the individual in question doesn't run on the same rails as everybody else.

Thaddeus comes to mind when thinking of "rig," because he was a particularly eccentric town character. In his heyday, Thaddeus would appear on the street sporting a gold hard hat with deer antlers glued on either side. Stuck on each of the antler points was an orange Styrofoam ball. Picture that. With this headgear, the hair and beard of a biblical prophet, a ragged barn coat, and an ever-present ripe smell, Thaddeus would approach tourists and say huffily, "Wish I had your money!"

He was tolerated and deemed harmless, however. Agreement to this was expressed by saying "What a *rig,* that Thaddeus!"

Another Vermont trait is a wry sense of humor, an outlook really, that is shaped by irony and often by struggle, and by a path in life sometimes twisted and not, as Frost said, the one always taken. Wry is even used to describe the "crooked" grin that goes with that outlook, and I've seen many a Vermonter with that grin over the years. It says they've seen life turn bottom-side up and go in the ditch, but they're still game to get the wreck back on the road and shift it into go-forward. Shoot, you *need* a sense of humor if you're going to boil sap enough to refill Lake Willoughby, just to get a gallon of syrup. You *need* that humor if you're going to grow tomatoes during a summer so short it starts on Sunday and ends on Saturday. Sometimes it takes that wry humor just to drive home at night through that war zone of potholes and frost heaves we in Vermont call a highway.

I'm almost done, because Vermonters are *supposed* to be laconic. They're also decent, kindly folk. I won't dwell on this, because it would embarrass most Vermonters, but if you were around when Irene blew in back in 2011, you'll know what I mean. Neighbors who were flooded out, were flooded with casseroles. Up on the headwaters of the White River, towns like Rochester and Pittsfield were cut off, but Vermonters rode four-wheelers over the mountain to bring medicine, food, and more help. Vermonters help their neighbors and strangers, too. I'll bet more than one reader here has been pulled out of a snowy ditch by a Vermonter who waved and drove off when the motorist started pulling bills out of a purse or wallet.

A real Vermont Farmer is someone who gets up in town meeting and identifies himself or herself as a farmer and no one laughs.

Finally, a true Vermonter loves the Green Mountains like no other place on earth. If the beauty of these hills during the rest of the year isn't enough, think of all those maples in the fall when they catch fire, red and orange and gold. That kind of beauty gets in your blood. This love of the land and the Vermont outlook can be shared by in-staters and out-of-staters alike. If you like what you've read here, you're a Vermonter at heart; I don't care if you're from Boston or Brattleboro. If you heart Vermont, every once in a while you'll lift your head and gaze into the distance, off to the ridgelines above our small valleys. You'll breathe in deeply and maybe you'll smell clover, and maybe you'll smell cow manure, but either way, you'll be intoxicated, and right then you'll say, "By God, this is the place for me."

There's NO difference because...

"The minute you get up in the
morning, you're on the job."

(Idea lifted from Slappy White)

CHAPTER 9

Department of Subtlety and Nuance

This potpourri chapter of one-liners, non sequiturs, stray cats, and axioms will, we hope, show Vermont's abiding antipathy for self-promoters and grandstanders. In the Green Mountains, there are two categories of people: those who do the work, and those who grab (or accept) the credit. Severe judgments or indictments are not meant; this is just the way the world works.

What is the difference among:

Being quarantined
Being retired
Being unemployed
Aging in place?

☛ Answer left.

Irreverent, witty, and sometimes obtuse, Vermont State Senator Mark MacDonald (D-Orange) employs the best of Vermont understatement to track his prey. He's strategic, but not cruel. For example, Senator MacDonald will politely advise: "Never murder an adversary who is busy trying to hang himself." Right out of the James Carville school of "If your opponent is drowning, throw 'im an anvil." ➡

Ezra was disconsolate when he realized that the family fridge weren't gonna compost in his lifetime.

Invoking the "Mercy Rule" on the state senate floor, more than once MacDonald kindly urged a fellow senator: ➡

When you find yourself deep in a hole...

the first thing to do is STOP DIGGING

Bill Mares's father lived by this corollary: ⬇

The Steam That Toots the Whistle Never Turned a Wheel

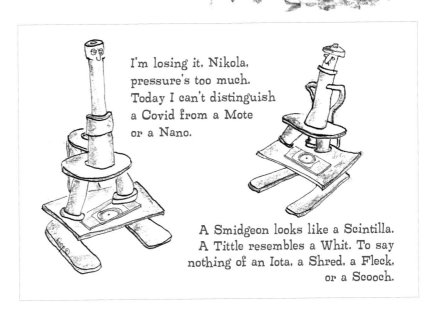

Trampolining off the postulate that "everyone is entitled to an opinion, but not her own set of facts," Vermonters can get downright playful with their data, but don't tamper with the truth of it. ➡

I'm losing it, Nikola, pressure's too much. Today I can't distinguish a Covid from a Mote or a Nano.

A Smidgeon looks like a Scintilla. A Tittle resembles a Whit. To say nothing of an Iota, a Shred, a Fleck, or a Scooch.

On the House Ways and Means Committee, Chairman Oreste Valsangiacomo chronically wrangled with "TACKS" reform: ↓

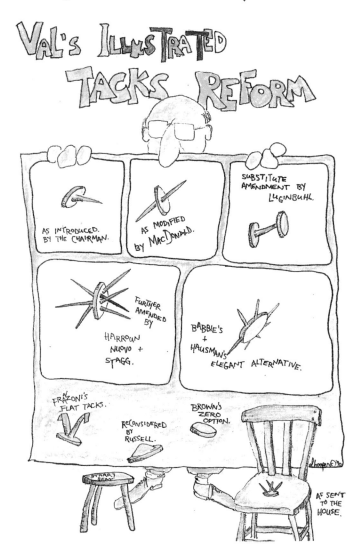

Vermonters are logical. Deduction is in their DNA. ↓

"Doctors have determined that birthdays ar good for your health."

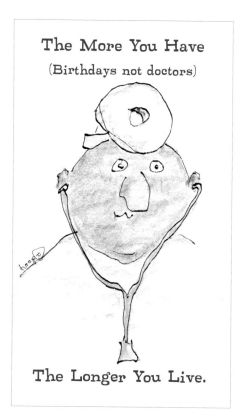

TODAY'S TEASER:

Who is Willy Nilly?
And why is he always
behind the Eight Ball?

Even in Vermont, the ubiquitous ZOOM gatherings have replaced old tech. ➡

Mostly, Vermonters of every station approach work methodically. ➡

One's first impulse in politics
often goes like this: ⬇

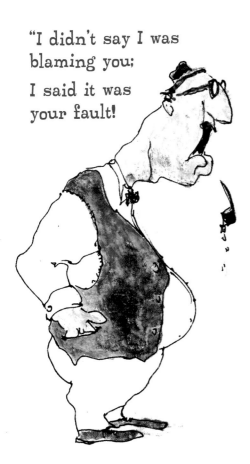

"I didn't say I was
blaming you;
I said it was
your fault!

But Norbert would advise on
Valentine's Day, with a Vermont twist . . . ↗

some
Valentines
Day
advice:

FORGIVE
YOUR
ENEMIES.

nuthin'
makes 'em
So Mad.

You don't need a parachute
to skydive...

You only need a parachute
to skydive twice.

Wise Father Mares cautions again: ⬇

Norbert ignores the
minor errors as he sweeps
toward the Grand Fallacy.

MAVIS MAELSTROM

Even normally generous Vermonters can mete out spontaneous humorous retribution after enduring a lifetime of abuse from a virago.

Mavis Maelstrom, of Manchester, was known for her rudeness. She seldom—well, never actually—said a pleasant word about or to anyone. When people saw her striding up Main Street in her housedress and trademark red wool sweater, they steered clear of the abuse she would surely administer.

Some years later, at Mavis's open-casket funeral, the sweetest man in the world, Charlie Cheermeister, delivered retribution. A longtime target of Mavis's derisive invective, Charlie opined, in more than a stage whisper, to the congregants: "I see Mavis is wearing her red sweater; well, she won't be needin' *that* where *she's* goin'!"

NORBERT PUTS ANOTHER NAIL IN THE COFFIN

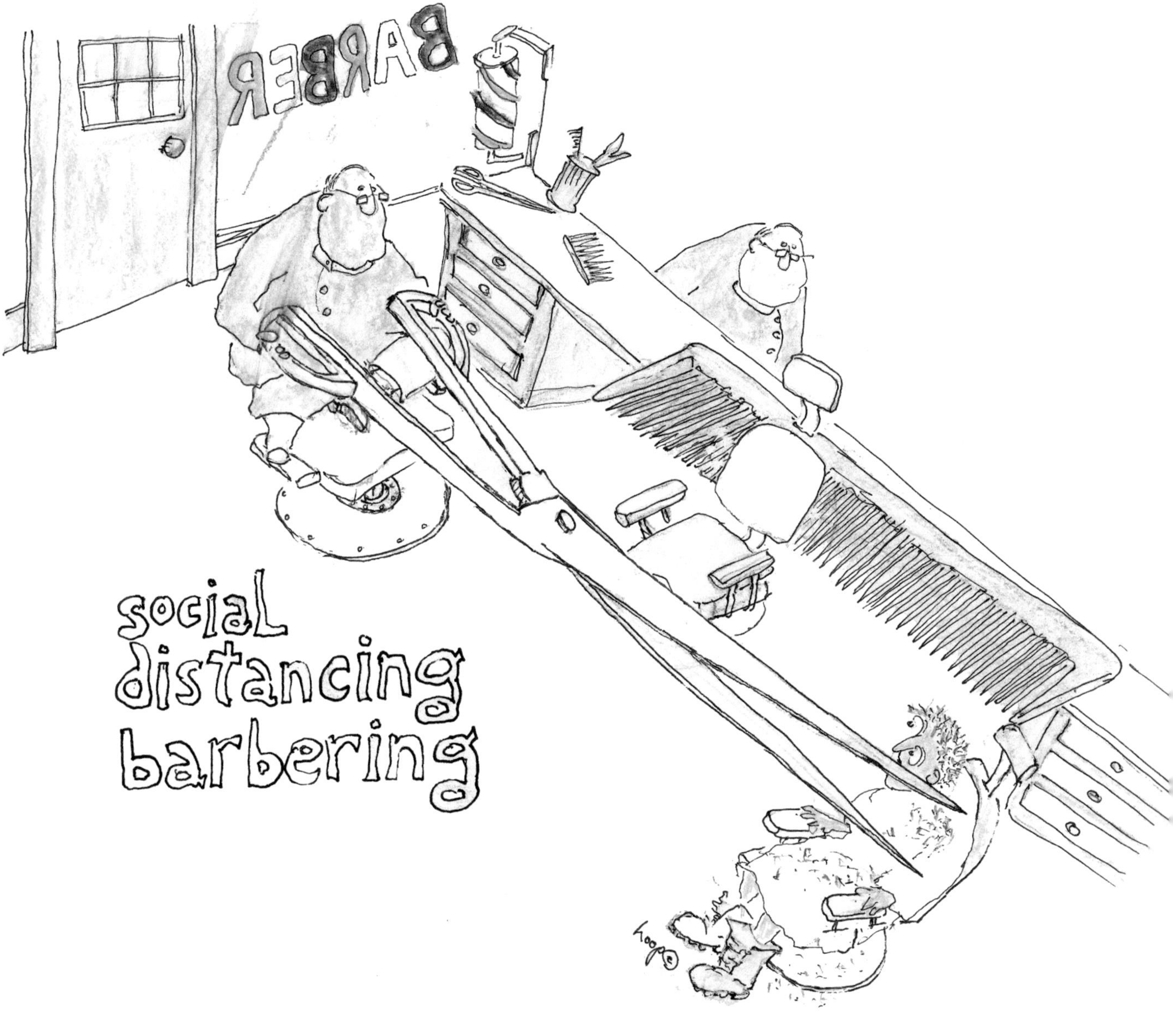
BARBER
social distancing barbering

CHAPTER 10

Improv and Sketch Comedy

Afunny thing happened to Vermont humor in the 21st century— well, several funny things—it went on stage and gender equity won the day. Across the state in bars, at non-profit benefits, in front of fraternal organizations, and in school gyms, aspiring comedians peddled their witty wares. It wasn't quite Borscht Belt style, but the inspirations were national: *Saturday Night Live,* the late shows, *The Daily Show, Comedy Central.* This was performance humor.

Dozens of people tried out this performance humor, from rankest amateurs to the most serious of aspiring professionals. They all found they liked the public display of making folks laugh by being yourself! Each took a different path, singly or in groups.

And, it was led by women.

By general agreement, the founder of Vermont's local comedy scene was Josie Leavitt.[46]

Leavitt started doing stand-up comedy in 1993, and gigged regularly at comedy clubs such as Caroline's on Broadway and the Comedy Cellar in her native New York City. In 1996, she moved to Vermont with her then-partner, Elizabeth Bluemle, to open the Flying Pig Bookstore in Charlotte. For twenty years Leavitt worked at the store, which has since moved to Shelburne Village. It took her nearly a decade to get back into stand-up.

But when she did, she was a dynamo. In 2005, she debuted a semi-regular stand-up series, called "Stand Up, Sit Down, and Laugh," which featured almost exclusively local comics. In 2006 she founded The Divas, an all-female, five-member troupe. At about the same time, Leavitt began teaching stand-up, primarily through the Flynn Center for the Performing Arts. She went further, to teach in a women's prison, at a hangout for homeless youth, and to cancer survivors, like herself.

One homeless teen, she recalls, joked about what it's like to "wake up on the wrong side of the sidewalk." Another, when asked to describe homelessness to someone who's never experienced it, said, "It's like never, *ever* having toilet paper."

"It gives them a chance to reframe an event in their life," said Leavitt. "Making light of a personal tragedy is often the first step toward putting it behind them and moving on."

Her recurring lesson/advice/ mantra in all her classes was: "I would tell them that you can have a bad day, and you can have a funny day. But guess what? They're the same day."

"The optimist believes we live in the Best of all Possible Worlds.

The pessimist fears that may be true."
—G.B. Shaw

A FISHING STORY

by Josie Leavitt

My family is strange and estranged. I haven't seen my uncle or two cousins since my father's third wedding, when I was seventeen. Now I'm forty-five, so clearly it's been some years since we've all gotten together. Finally, we decided to get together.

So, what does my uncle recommend? Shark fishing. I couldn't help but think that higher-functioning families do not go shark fishing when they haven't seen each other for almost thirty years. They have large BBQs— but no, we shark fish.

So, two weeks ago I packed up to go to Palm Beach, Florida, to shark fish. My uncle David, cousin Orin, and I were the fishermen. I fish every summer in Lake Champlain. Let me just say, tropical fish are not like lake fish. They fight and they fight hard. The little—I say "little" in comparison to a shark—fifteen pound fish I caught took fifteen minutes to get into the boat. It seems to me, fish down there swim faster and harder to get away.

I did catch a shark, but I almost lost him, because I was day dreaming in the warm sun and my hand was barely on the rod. Thank goodness I have fast reflexes, or not only would have lost the rod, I would have been in the water getting hauled around by a shark. I like to think I'm strong, but apparently I do not possess the arm strength one needs to make catching a shark fun. After ten minutes of fighting, and swearing, and seeing the shark take the line seemingly to a distant Caribbean island, I hunkered down and fought back. This was probably the only shark I'd ever get a chance to catch, so I was not going to give up, burning arms and all.

I didn't know that when you catch a shark he determines where you go on the boat. Just because I hooked him on the bow, didn't mean I wasn't going to traipse around the boat following his every move. Imagine trying to hold on to a rod in very rough water with an eighty pound shark—at this point I was thinking of him as the Beast-Monster—going left and right, over and around all sides of the boat. No one helped me with the shark. On this boat, you hook 'em, you reel 'em in.

The captain brought him up to the side of the boat, gaffed him (looks painful, but probably isn't), we took a bunch of pictures, I kissed the shark's rough head, and silently thanked him for bringing my family together. And then we let him go.

I fish every summer in Lake Champlain. Let me just say, tropical fish are not like lake fish.

KATHLEEN KANZ[47]

Kathleen Kanz came to Vermont in 1996 to work as a regional planner, but she'd always had a yen to be on stage and make folks laugh. While she "planned" at her day job, she performed scores of times all over Vermont in clubs, for public benefits, at birthday parties, political events, senior centers, assisted living communities, libraries, wineries, breweries, distilleries, an aerobics room, the Worcester outdoor farmer's market across the street from a cemetery . . .

In 2009, Kathleen Kanz founded the Green Mountain Comedy Festival in Burlington. She said, "Nobody was putting me on stage, so I put me on stage. Plus, I recruited local comics that I'd seen doing comedy at music open mic nights, and whose material I liked. Because my name was on my show (The Kathleen Kanz Comedy Hour), I knew I needed to be able to defend my choice of comic and material if someone didn't enjoy it. The next year I was hosting a quarterly show at the Black Door in Montpelier, and a monthly show at the Monkey House in Winooski. Once or twice, there might be a national headliner at the Flynn Theater. That's where I met Nathan Hartswick and his then-girlfriend (now spouse), Natalie Miller. I asked Nathan if he would videotape the show. He and Natalie did the tape, and we've known each other ever since."

In 2016, Kanz won Vermont's Funniest Comedian contest, as the first woman to do so. She describes her favorite humor as very compact jokes with twisted logic: "The first time I saw Steven Wright on *The Tonight Show* with Johnny Carson, I thought: *Oh, you can do it like that?*"

Some examples of Kathleen Kantz's comedy

I think déjà vu is nonsense, and it's not the first time I've thought that.

The Bible says the meek shall inherit the earth—boy is that gonna be a long line . . . but very easy to cut.

I find that living in Vermont lets me get extra wear out of my Fashion Don'ts.

Growing up in my little family, nobody was related. My sister and I were both adopted, and my parents, delightfully, were not related. *Huge win* for the home team—and we are very proud.

Generally, Mavis gets down the wreath by Easter.

An elder gentleman that I work with asked me: "Why nowadays do female mannequins have such noticeable nipples?" I told him, "It's because the store sets the air conditioning at fifty—it's freezing in there," and then I grabbed two workplace complaint forms—one for me and one for him—because I did not like his question and *he* did not like my answer, and we're gonna talk about it on Monday with HR.

As I walk through my life, it's become clear that two groups are drawn to me—elderly women and cats. They flock to me. They cross busy lines of traffic to get to me, and speak to me, because I think they find me comforting. It leads me to believe that I may have been an Afghan in a former life—perhaps a shawl. Does anybody out there knit or crochet? Do I seem at all familiar to you? I'm getting a vibe off someone out there. Someone out there has touched my wool in a former life, and I thank you, especially in this time of quarantine.

NATHAN HARTSWICK AND NATALIE MILLER[48]

Nathan Hartswick and Natalie Miller are a married couple who both grew up in the Northeast Kingdom of Vermont. From an early age, both Nathan and Natalie performed children's theater and music on stage. They say their childhood performances helped them develop their comedic timing. Their families were both demanding, but also very encouraging of their talents.

The couple produced their own shows across Vermont for many years, and always wanted to open their own comedy club. Their dream was not just for a venue, but also a community space. Ecumenically, they wanted to create a clubhouse of sorts, that comedians in Vermont could call home.

"When we first started, there weren't enough opportunities to perform," says Miller. "We always felt we should create our own opportunities." The couple says, when they first began producing shows in 2009, local audiences didn't have much experience with the interactivity of a live comedy show. They were used to sitting in silence at music concerts. "We had to 'coach' people to loosen up and laugh more," recalls Hartswick.

"We had to 'coach' people to loosen up and laugh more."

A national trend in stand-up comedy—and one the couple adhered to as they each developed as comedians—is to write from personal experience. "The humor is more original that way," says Miller, "and there is less of a chance you'll be accused of stealing someone else's jokes."

Joke by Nathan Hartswick:

I was an English major, so I notice the language people use. The other day somebody said to me, "I don't trust that guy as far as I can throw him."

I thought, why are we *throwing people, exactly?* I mean, by that logic, if someone could be easily thrown . . . they could be easily trusted. Right?

Babies, for example. Babies are not gonna tell your secrets *and* they're lightweight and aerodynamic. When you throw a baby, and it flies a hundred yards . . . that's a *trustworthy* baby, right there.

Joke by Natalie Miller:

My opinion is that ice cream is better than sex. Oh, you don't believe me? Well, let me ask you this: when was the last time you were eating a rich, delicious pint of Ben & Jerry's ice cream, and thought to yourself, "Ugh. When is *this* gonna be over?"

"My opinion is that ice cream is better than sex. Oh, you don't believe me?"

When they opened Vermont Comedy Club in 2015, Hartswick and Miller were riding a national boom in comedy. Their stated goal was to be a comedy club that was ahead of the curve.

"We've always preferred booking performers who are on their way up, rather than on their way down," Hartswick commented. Miller added that they work hard to achieve a gender balance in all of their shows.

At the comedy club, the couple also teaches classes in several forms of comedy: stand-up (written, solo material); sketch (written, group material); and improv (spontaneous group comedy). "We love to teach, and we are always so happy to see a performer make a breakthrough," says Miller.

Hartswick, who teaches mostly stand-up, feels that to be a good comedian "You just have to keep getting onstage and doing it, and be self-aware enough to admit what isn't working, so you can improve on it."

Community is very important to the couple. "Comedy can be competitive, and we want Vermont comedians to celebrate each other's successes," says Hartswick. Each year, Hartswick and Miller produce comedian barbecues, holiday parties, and festivals, in order keep the community connected. Says Miller, "We're all in this for the same reason: we just want to make people laugh."

RICHARD BOWEN[49]

Although he was a manic skateboarder for eighteen years, comedian Richard Bowen insists he is not a "skateboard comic." As he said, "Both do make you look at the world in a different way. There's much trial and error in both activities. You fall a lot, but in stand-up, there's no physical risk."

Since early 2014, Bowen has been writing jokes and performing across the country. His style, an offbeat mix of shy demeanor and a relentless forward push of dry comic persona, fosters both carefree and very precise jokes. All are memorized, but he's flexible in taking down different jokes from the shelf. He likes short jokes, word plays, rhythm, and alliteration.

He writes stuff down *all the time*. He has now collected over one hundred notebooks of random jokes. The best ones wind up in his sets and his handwritten 'zine, "Rich Jokes." He distributes the latter wherever he performs, and the first twelve issues are available as a box set.

Born in South Carolina, Bowen attended high school in the Northeast Kingdom before graduating from Johnson State College with a degree in studio art. After a host of odd jobs, he entered a drop-in improv jam at Spark Arts, a local performing arts studio.

In 2018, Bowen hit a sort of big time when he won the title of the Laffy Taffy candy's first "Chief Laugh Officer," whose duties were vague, but whose prize money of ten thousand dollars was green. Three of his submissions were:

Did you hear about the spider cow?

It had eight calves.

What do you call a flooded movie theater?

A dive-in.

Why did the psychic turn down a piece of candy?

She had a bad filling.

"With social media, I know that a lot of people think I'm just out there skating and doing stand-up," he says. "People always think I'm making a living at it, but I'm not."

"He's the hardest-working comedian I know—at any level," says Vermont Comedy Club co-owner Natalie Miller.

Nathan Hartswick, her partner and VCC co-owner, adds, "We lay claim to him as a Vermont comedian because this is generally home base for him, but he is often traveling all over the world, and *always* performing comedy—if there is a mic there, he will tell jokes. Very unique guy with a likable one-liner style."

More Bowen Jokes:

Got a new microwave just for cookin' hot dogs. It's a Frank Zappa.

Scorpions have to be really careful if the back of their head itches.

The first step to quitting a job is admitting that you have one.

You shouldn't steal other people's jokes. Take it from me!

To all the people who have never been remembered:
You will never be forgotten.

I'm an egomaniac with an inferiority complex.
But nobody's perfect and a lot of the time I feel like I'm nobody.

Bees have fur; can bees get fleas?

I wanted to give up on cave painting, but I decided to give it one Lascaux.

An animation of Jesus is a GIF from God.

I never trust a menu with the sides in the middle.

Elbows are the knuckles of arms.

"You shouldn't steal other people's jokes. Take it from me!"

Oh, and here is my favorite Vermont joke I ever wrote: I tell jokes all over the state. One time I got booked for a gig, and when they told me where it was, I bought a gun! I thought the show was gonna be in the middle of Barre. But the show was in Middlebury. So I left the gun at home and I just brought my contempt for rich white people.

TINA FRIML[50]

A different kind of cringe comedy comes from Tina Friml, a graduate of Saint Michael's College in Colchester, Vermont.

"Comedy became a cool thing, then it became a hobby, then it became my life," Tina Friml told the College magazine. Friml took her first comedy class, won Vermont's Funniest Comedian, performed in Montreal's famous Just For Laughs (one of the most prestigious comedy festivals in the world), and got signed by a New York City manager all within three years of graduating from Saint Michael's.

Friml has cerebral palsy and is making a comedic career of it.

"My jokes are not about me being disabled. They're about people reacting to me being disabled," she says. "It's like putting up a mirror to the audience, and showing them what I see.

"I learned pretty quickly that disability was, is, and always will be a taboo topic to joke about—even coming out of the mouth of a disabled person. People will always be hesitant to laugh out loud. No one wants to feel like they're punching down. Sometimes I'd say something degrading against myself, and it's met with more 'Awww's than laughter. However, the one thing people absolutely love to laugh at is themselves.

"That's the simple answer. The more elaborate answer is that, to quote something I say all the time, I don't suffer from CP. I live with CP. I suffer from people. The majority of my comedy regarding disability is about things other people have said or thought about me, because in reality, that's the majority of the problem. So, holding that figurative mirror up is catering to both myself and the audience: It puts the audience at ease and in a more comfortable position to laugh, and it also allows me to air out my grievances for how others treat me."

> "Hi, I'm Tina, and I'm disabled. But don't worry, you're going to be okay."

From one of Tina's comedy transcripts:

Hi, I'm Tina, and I'm disabled. But don't worry, you're going to be okay. I mean, I'm kind of disabled. Not really though. I'm kind of half-and-half. I'm not fully committed to this lifestyle. I'm like the bisexuality of ability. I'm bi-able, or 'bibled.' And so, I'm a bit of an enigma, right? Like, people see me and they don't know what's happening. They don't know what to say, but that doesn't stop them.

So I get a lot of weird things said to me. Like, back when I was in high school, in art school painting a color wheel and a girl next to me said,

"You know, Tina. It's so cool. You're disabled but you're actually good at stuff."

"You know, Tina. It's so cool. You're disabled but you're actually good at stuff. I know, right? What do you say to that?! That is a common misconception, Becky. It's not that I'm actually good at all this stuff. I'm just particularly bad at being disabled.

How dare she. I am very bad at many things. This top button took me forty minutes. I tell you, if you ever catch me with this button undone, you know that I was running late that morning. It was just this or breakfast. And let's be honest. I'd rather look a bit thirsty than hungry.

I do have other jokes, by the way . . . I will ask this, though. If anyone comes in the room from now on, nobody tell them that I'm disabled. They are late, and don't deserve the context.

Just say that I'm foreign, okay? And you could really milk that, too. Be like, 'Yeah, what do you think of that cute foreign comedian? She seemed like she was a bit slo . . . venian to me . . .'

A little more about me. I'm twenty-six. It's a good age, the oldest I've ever been. Being twenty-six is a bit of a threshold. People stop asking whether or not I'm in college. You would know if I didn't go to college, right? 'Cause I'd be something like a supervisor at Chili's. But I did! I actually got my degree in journalism.

So, I'm a waitress at Chili's.

I do comedy just to show you that I'm just like you. Like, I have good days and bad days. And well, whenever I do have a bad day and I want to disappear, I go out. I go to the bar! Not to drink but to be around other people who have been drinking. I just blend right in. I go out a lot, and I usually judge a club based on what they think I'm on. I admit, I am kind of a trick question to bouncers, I'm a bit of a riddle. My mouth says booze, but my hands say cocaine. What am I?

The moral of all this, if you will, is that being born disabled turned out to be the best decision that I ever made. Everything that I do is 'an inspiration.'

Like, why do you think I can get up here in front of you and do this so confidently? I *know* that even if I bomb and no one laughs, it's still, like, a Ted Talk."

> "…We could argue many performers are professional even if they don't get paid."

STEALING FROM WORK[51]

Stealing from Work is a sketch comedy show founded by Angie Albeck and Marianne DiMasco in 2012.

"We met at work. We realized we had a similar sense of humor. I [Marianne] had just performed in Canada at the Fringe Festival and had the opportunity to see amazing sketch comedy. I returned to work and looked around for potential writing partners. Angie was the clear choice. She is smart and very funny."

"When Marianne asked me [Angie] if I had any interest in writing sketch comedy, I knew I was woefully underqualified to work with her. I had seen her perform skillfully in several productions, and I was incredibly impressed with a play she had co-written, called *Seeking*. I hadn't been involved in any theater to speak of since college, but Marianne assured me that she had some writing exercises we could try, and that it would all be in good fun.

"We had applied for a grant to develop our first show. We found ourselves writing about a variety of Vermont themes. A deadline was on the horizon for us to decide on a name for our troupe. There was a recent trend in Vermont, of people embezzling funds. We decided on the name 'Stealing from Work.' It actually has nothing to do with us working together. We could fill a troupe twelve times over with all of the talent in Vermont. Our team is comprised of: two writers, Angie and Marianne; director Seth Jarvis; sound designer/stage manager/film editor Jess Wilson; actors Alex Hudson, Amy Halpin Riley, Chris Caswell, Geeda Searfoorce, Jory Raphael, and Marianne."

✦

Given the chance to interview the pair myself, I recorded the following:

What comedic education have you had? We have taken classes through Second City, Montreal Improv, and The Assembly.

Can you describe your comedic style? I think we have a satirical, feminist, silly, physical, musical, fart-joke-loving style. It's fairly eclectic. We have been compared to *Portlandia,* because of how we treat Vermont as a character in some sketches.

With all of our humor, we make sure we are "punching up" or "punching in." A favorite subject for our satire is ourselves, and the groups of which we are a part. Who better to criticize us than us?

Where do you place yourselves on the spectrum from amateur to professional? This is a tough question to answer. Stealing from Work doesn't pay any of our bills, but we pay members of the troupe a stipend, as well as a percentage share of any profits. I guess this makes us professional. Although, we could argue many performers are professional even if they don't get paid.

And their message? We often interrogate and criticize ourselves and the groups of which we are a part. Our audiences often share these group affiliations, so we hope that people walk away feeling like it is okay to laugh at jokes about farts and body parts, and also that it is okay to think critically about our world and our places in it.

We are most satisfied when people describe us the way this audience member did: "Witty, hilarious physical comedy that took wonderful satirical swipes at our smug sense of liberal culture, our current dysfunctional politics, and perceptions of gender." Also, fart jokes.

Stealing from Work bit:

Willie: Welcome to *Race Against the Clock,* the exciting new game show where contestants race against their biological clocks to have a baby before it's too late.

Caroline: Wait. What?

Willie: Today's prizes include a fabulous home egg freezing system! Extract and store your reproductive material in the comfort of your own home. You'll be over the moon knowing your ova are waiting as you squander your baby making years working sixty hours a week while also pursuing your online MBA.

Caroline: I thought this was the show where I guess the cost of a car.

Willie: And the runner-up will receive this handsome travel mug with *Race Against the Clock*'s catchphrase "The last one in's a rotten egg!" Here's your first challenge: Tell me, Caroline, at what age will you have to meet "Mr. Right" in order to have any chance of having a baby with him?

The problem with the rat race is:
Even if you win, you are still a rat.

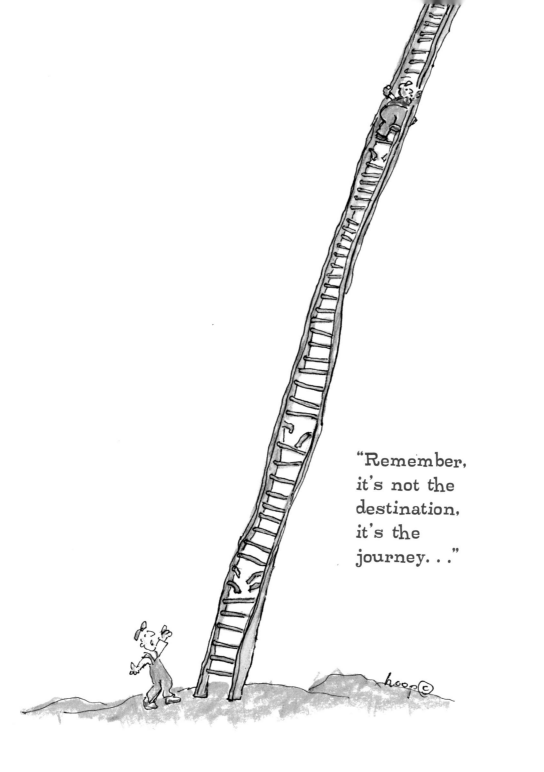

"Remember, it's not the destination, it's the journey..."

CHAPTER 11

Almost Home

by Don Hooper

I swooned when Bill Mares asked me to "have at it" in the last chapter. Bill said, "Hoops, tell us what drives you, your big themes, your passions—and why humor? What's the deal with that?"

Mares went on: "If you can, just say your story in pictures with a modicum of explanation. Remember what they say in politics: when you're explaining, you're losing." I think I may "lose" here, but what the hey, Mares anointed me chief of this chapter.

To cope with life's struggles, Garrison Keillor names his Minnesota lake Wobegon

Now that I got your Attention, here's the deal!

(as in, Woe, Be Gone). To the South African folk tale *Abiyoyo,* Pete Seeger applied his banjo and humor-filled storytelling to dispose of the menacing giant and repatriate the ukulele lad and his magic-dispensing dad. Similarly, Mares and I have resorted to humor to subvert our difficulties.

I like to ask two not-particularly-profound questions about almost everything.

The first is: "So what?"

The other is: "How well?"

These are benign questions provoked mostly by annoyingly incurable curiosity. But these two questions can produce unexpectedly humorous (though usually not laugh-out-loud) results; such as the subtle, understated, though occasionally slapstick, Vermont humor we've tried to share in this book.

Here's an example:

From birth, I evinced some decently progressive DNA. As the only "European" student attending an all-Ceylonese, two-thousand-student secondary school in Sri Lanka, I overcame my fear of being a minority of one.

For three years, from 1968 to 1971, I taught biology, bricklaying, and development studies in the Peace Corps in Botswana, southern Africa. There, I learned again that if you're poor, it may have everything to do with where you are born, and nothing to do with your competence and work ethic.

Fifty years later, my Harvard College roommate, professor physician Ron Bogdasarian, would crystallize a guiding lifelong principle for me:

"No one really *cares* how much you *know*... until they *know* how much you *care.*"

Since reading Bill McKibben's *The End of Nature* on my honeymoon with Allison Hooper in 1989, I became obsessed with the climate catastrophe we are blithely creating for our children.

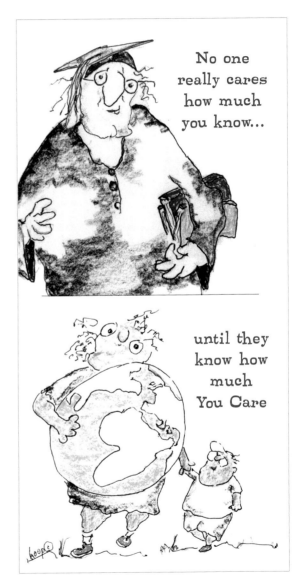

The cartoons aren't exactly hilarious. But they do represent my goofy attempt to lighten heavy topics by viewing them through the naïve lens of a sort of hapless Hiram or Norbert character.

Even as a Vermont back-to-the-land immigrant, my overarching concerns remained international. I made my maiden speech in 1985 on the Vermont House floor on the need, morally and practically, to divest our state workers' and teachers' pension funds from businesses doing business in odious Apartheid South Africa. With the collapse of the Soviet Union in 1990, I pondered how the US would now be able to divert its bloated military budget to butter instead of guns.

◆

When our Barnyard Chorus fresh goat milk business evolved into the Vermont Butter & Cheese Co., I invented a clumsy cameo character,

after the cold war:

military spending: progressive version

Without fail, Ezra checked everyday to see if his Peace Dividend had arrived.

Chester, who could be found toiling over a cauldron oozing with ooze. Chester regularly reappeared with captions such as:

"There are three basic rules for making cheese. Unfortunately, nobody knows what they are."
Or,
"When will you be done, Chester?"
Chester replies: "Feta Accompli."

As philosophical, monkey-wrencher, naturalist Edward Abbey said, "Society is like a stew. If we don't stir it up once in a while, then a layer of scum floats to the top." To which Chester would say, "And the *bottom* gets burnt!"

Meanwhile, in the Creamery, Allison would be dragging around a ten-gallon milk can asking provocatively: "Seen Trump's budget?" before unloading her derision, "He's all guns and no butter."

Crazy to reduce my complicity in cooking the planet, I scarf up cute ideas whenever they sprout. Here's an electric vehicle simile that clean energy guru Linda McGinnis offered from the podium at a climate conference: 🖐

See Trump's budget?... all guns and no butter.

Driving a Tesla is like...

driving a really big Smart phone.

"The Steaks Have Never been Higher" applies to just about every election cycle, and to mega-stress catastrophes like the Covid-19 pandemic and global warming.

✦

My dear, departed mother, Marion Hooper, bestowed on her five children several good habits. Before the age of the internet, Mother loved to stay in genuine, personal touch with far-flung friends on several distant continents. Her mantra: "It takes letters to get letters." One Christmas, I gave her a box of letterhead featuring her caricature (see below).

On cynical days, I quip: "Remember, we're all in this ALONE." But that forlorn fatalism arouses a flurry of more assertive retorts: "Relationships Matter; Stay in Touch" and "Don't Whine, Organize."

City Year, an inspiring Boston non-profit, sets the bar humorously low with its motto: "We don't make things worse." Dennis Eckersley rants from the play-by-play booth atop Fenway Park, "Just put the ball in-play, dang-it. Good things can happen then." John Lewis urges us to "Make Good Trouble." Following those modest admonitions, I find fulfillment attempting to practice five basics:

• Love like it matters.

• Be Kind. (One kind act a day is doable and feels great!)

• Be insatiably Curious (it might even postpone Alzheimers).

• Puzzle (think outside the box; we're gonna need creative resolve to subvert the Climate Crisis).

• Embrace Humor — which is why Bill cobbled up these yarns and I enjoyed coloring them.

So you think Climate Change
is a bad thing?

ENDNOTES

[1] Allen R. Foley, *What the Old-Timer Said*, Brattleboro: Stephen Greene Press (1971): 58.

[2] Robert Davis, *Vermont Laughter* (1940): 29-30.

[3] Vrest Orton, *The Unique Inauguration of Calvin Coolidge* (August 3, 1923): 11.

[4] *Vermont Life* (Summer 1986): 58.

[5] Ibid.

[6] After growing by only 12 percent in ninety years (1860-1950), Vermont's population jumped 32 percent by 1980.

[7] Alan J. Keays, "Funny Bones," *Rutland Herald Sunday Magazine* (August 27, 1997).

[8] Robert C. Davis, *Vermont Laughter:* 5-6.

[9] Walter Hard, *Walter Hard's Vermont People*, Middlebury: Vermont Books (1941).

[10] Robert C. Davis, *Vermont Laughter.*

[11] Allen R. Foley, *What the Old Timer Said*, Brattleboro: Stephen Greene Press (1971): 22-23.

[12] Ibid., 28.

[13] bid., 18.

[14] Thomas C. Mann & Janet Greene, *Over Their Dead Bodies*, Brattleboro: Stephen Green Press (1962).

[15] Bill Mares, *Burlington Free Press* (January 13, 1978).

[16] E. Donald Asselin, *New England Laughs*, Middlebury: Vermont Books (1963): 22.

[17] I bid., 75-76.

[18] Ibid., 31-32.

[19] Allen R. Foley, *What the Old Timer Said*, Brattleboro: Stephen Greene Press (1971): 29.

[20] Vrest Orton, *Vermont Afternoons with Robert Frost*, Charles Tuttle: Rutland (1982). Printed with permission.

[21] Christopher Klyza and Stephen C. Trombulak, *The Story of Vermont: A Natural and Cultural History*, Lebanon: University Press of N.E. (1999): 108-109.

[22] Francis Colburn, *Letters Home and Further Indiscretions*, Shelburne: New England Press (1978): 60-61.

[23] In "Goats," we published this story under the title "Real Vermonters Don't Indulge in Disingenuous Greetings."

[24] Keith Jennison, *Vermont is Where You Find It*, New York: Harcourt. Brace & Co. 1941, : 84-6.

[25] E. Donald Asselin, *New England Laughs*, Middlebury (1963): 19.

[26] Ibid., 51-52.

[27] Ibid., 54-55.

[28] Loudon Young, *Off Main St., West Glover, VT*, Barton: The Chronicle (1977).

[29] Bill Mares, *Burlington Free Press* (January 13, 1978).

[30] *Vermont Sunday Magazine* (Rutland Herald), October 21, 1990.

[31] Deane Davis, *Nothing But the Truth*, Shelburne: New England Press, (1982): 82.

[32] Still a better slogan than that of the Texas politician of Bill's upbringing, who asserted, "Honesty is no Substitute for Experience."

[33] He was not alone. In fact, only two of the several thousand troops aboard drowned.

[34] FYI—in haying, which is Vermont's principal summer occupation, there are four steps. First you *mow* the timothy, orchard grass, alfalfa, or whatever. Then you *tedd* it, to break up the stems and allow it to dry faster. *Tedding* is scrambling up the drying grass with a PTO-driven egg-beater-like *tedder* implement behind your fifty-year-old Ford 8-N utility tractor. Third, you *rake* the hay into windrows, so you can *bale* it efficiently,

which is step four. Finally, you march the wagonload of bales up the elevator into the haymow in your barn.

[35] Bob Stannard, *How to Survive the Recession,* Manchester: Shires Press (2010).

[36] Vermont Public Radio (March 16, 2016).

[37] Vermont Public Radio (May 25, 2009).

[38] *The Winooski* (November 22, 2019).

[39] David Budbill, "Bugs in a Bowl" from *Moment to Moment: Poems of a Mountain Recluse.* Copyright © 1999 by David Budbill. Reprinted with the permission of The Permissions Company, LLC on behalf of Copper Canyon Press, copper-canyonpress.org.

[40] unpublished Historicity of Avery's Gore manuscript by Outsider's Inc. / Danny Gore / Norman L. Lewis

[41] Ibid

[42] We're indebted to Pamela Polston, of *Seven Days,* for some of this "review."

[43] Thanks to Paula Routly of *Seven Days* and Jim Lowe of the *Rutland Herald.*

[44] Rusty DeWees, *Scrawlins Too,* Morrisville: Rusty D. Inc (2011): 229-230.

[45] *Esquire* magazine January 1, 1984 (no page#)

[46] https://www.josieleavittcomedy.com

[47] https://kathleenkanz.com/

[48] https://www.vermontcomedyclub.com

[49] Jordan Adams, *Seven Days VT,* "Comedian Richard Bowen Just Wants to Tell Jokes Full Time" (July 18, 2018).

[50] https://www.tinafriml.com/biography

[51] Brent Hallenback, "Stealing from Work comedy group mines 'existential angst' in new show, 'From Russia with Likes'" *Burlington Free Press* (February 3, 2020).

So that's that, Diligent reader.

For you, we've pulled out ALL the STOPS.

CONTRIBUTORS

Bill Boardman of Woodstock, Vermont, began doing improvisational skits at the Yale Drama School in the 1960s. Soon after he moved to Vermont, in the early 1970s, he became a drama teacher at Woodstock Country School, from which he'd graduated in 1956, and about which he would write a 500-page history. He was also an assistant judge and a long-time "stringer" for the *Rutland Herald* newspaper. He formed an improvisation group called the Panther Players, which did live performances around the state, and even had a stint on Vermont Public Radio.

Julie A. Davis has over 40 years of combined experience in working with federal, state and local government entities, media, grant writing, and nonprofit development. Notable assignments include her seven year involvement with progressive electoral politics as an appointee under the administrations of former mayors Bernie Sanders and Peter Clavelle. She was a public policy coordinator for the Vermont Businesses for Social Responsibility and was instrumental in passing legislation for the creation of the Sustainable Jobs Fund. She also co-founded a nonprofit workforce development organization where she is currently employed. She obtained her MPA from the University of Vermont and is certified as a Law Clerk with the Vermont Bar Association. A native of Vermont she currently resides at her farmhouse in Cambridge, Vermont.

Peter Gilbert served as director of the Vermont Humanities Council 2002–2018. Prior to that, he taught English and a senior elective on constitutional law at Phillips Academy in Andover, Massachusetts, was Senior Assistant to the President of Dartmouth College and Associate Provost, and was a litigator at the Boston firm of Hale and Dorr. Peter's clear and articulate voice was well known throughout Vermont and beyond as a frequent commentator for Vermont Public Radio.

Adam Hall is the founder and editor of The Winooski, a local on-line satire site he founded in 2017. It has been featured on many other sites, including The Good Men Project and The Huffington Post. In addition to being a writer, he is also a trained opera singer, voice teacher, church musician, housing educator, vocal coach, husband, father, huge nerd, and stand-up comedian. Often all at once.

Alec Hastings grew up in the foothills of Vermont's Upper Connecticut River Valley. His early schooling came from farmers, loggers, and storytelling elders. Eventually, he met some fine teachers in Vermont College's Adult Degree Program, where he received degrees in creative writing and African American literature. A high school teacher by trade, Hastings is the author of the 2013 adventure novel, *Otter St. Onge and the Bootleggers,* set on Lake Champlain during Vermont's Prohibition. He currently lives with his beloved wife, Denise Martin, in Randolph Center, Vermont.

Walter Hard was a fifth-generation Vermonter and with his wife, was co-owner of the Johnny Appleseed Bookstore in Manchester, Vermont. Hard was a state legislator for five terms and a newspaper columnist for forty years. He died in 1966.

Willem Lange was born in 1935. A child of deaf parents, he grew up speaking sign language and first came to New England to attend prep school in 1950, as an alternative to reform school in his native New York state. He earned a degree at the College of Wooster in Ohio. In between those scattered semesters, he worked as a ranch hand, Adirondack guide, preacher, construction laborer, bobsled run announcer, assembly line worker, cab driver, bookkeeper, bartender, school teacher, contractor, newspaper and radio commentator, and publisher of nine books, among other things. For forty years, he and his wife Ida lived in New Hampshire, until they moved to Vermont in 2007 (http://willemlange.com).

Josie Leavitt is an award-winning comic who has been performing stand-up for longer than she can remember. Getting her start in New York City in the 1990s, she played at Stand-Up NY, Caroline's, the Comic Strip and many other clubs. Learn more at her website, josieleavittcomedy.com.

John McCullough of North Bennington, Vermont, was a banker, philanthropist, and grandson of Vermont Governor John G. McCullough.

Stephen Morris of Randolph, Vermont, is a consultant, writer, publisher, author of six books about Vermont, and co-founder of The Public Press. Himself an immigrant, he penned this article for the *Rutland Herald* about how Flatlanders could understand the locals.

Prof. David K. Smith of Pittsford and Middlebury taught economics at Middlebury College for almost 40 years and was much beloved by fellow faculty members and students alike. He served on the Vermont Council of Economic Advisors under four state governors, was a trustee of the village of Middlebury and as a consultant for Central Vermont Public Service. Smith played the bass fiddle, was an avid skier, and delighted those who knew him with his irrepressible humor. He died in 2006.

Bob Stannard is an eighth-generation Vermonter who worked as a logger, lobbyist, real estate broker, state legislator, newspaper columnist, and musician. He had the privilege to play with two "Kings," B.B. and Stephen, as well as other important blues musicians. He's recorded three albums and written two volumes of Swiftian satire about Vermont.

Louden Young was known throughout his life for his storytelling talent. During the 1970s, he began writing a column for *The Chronicle* based on his everyday experiences. A compilation of the columns was published in 1977, titled "Loudon Young, Off Main Street, West Glover VT." Young also sold advertising for the paper for years. He passed in 2004.

Remember we are all in this alone.

In kindergarten, **Don Hooper** was slow to master coloring inside the lines. But with two Harvard degrees, Hooper was never dismissed as the hapless goof he caricatures himself to be in his drawings. A Peace Corps teacher in Botswana, a back-to-the-land Vermont immigrant goat milker, legislator, Secretary of State, ardent enviro, …
Don revels in the good fortune life has dropped in his lap so far. He and his wife Allison (co-founder of Vermont Creamery) are nurtured by their three entrepreneurial lads, Miles, Sam, and Jay, and Miles' wife Daryll, all of whom live within a ten-mile bike ride of the Hoopers' Brookfield, Vermont homestead. Grandkids Olcott and Weston call Hoops "Mothusi," which means "helper," the generous nickname his students gave him in Botswana.

Raised in Texas, educated at Harvard, **Bill Mares** is a former journalist, state representative, and high school teacher. He has authored or co-authored 18 books on subjects ranging from the US Marines to desert travel, from war memorials to economic democracy, from brewing beer to beekeeping. Among Mares' books were four volumes of Vermont humor with University of Vermont professor Frank Bryan, one of which (*Out of Order*) was illustrated by Don Hooper. From 2007 to 2018, Mares wrote over 200 commentaries for Vermont Public Radio. He serves on the boards of VT Digger, the Vermont Beekeepers Association, the Vermont Brewers Association and Food4Farmers. He lives in Burlington, Vermont with his wife of 50 years, Chris Hadsel. They have two sons, Timothy and Nicholas.